MARRIAGE

MARRIAGE

100 STORIES AROUND INDIA'S FAVOURITE RITUAL

DEVDUTT PATTANAIK

Illustrations by the Author

RUPA

Published by
Rupa Publications India Pvt. Ltd 2021
7/16, Ansari Road, Daryaganj
New Delhi 110002

Sales Centres:

Allahabad Bengaluru Chennai
Hyderabad Jaipur Kathmandu
Kolkata Mumbai

Cover Illustration: Devdutt Pattanaik

ISBN: 978-93-5333-844-2

Second impression 2022

10 9 8 7 6 5 4 3 2

Designed and typeset in Garamond by Special Effects Graphics Design Co, Mumbai
Printed at HT Media Ltd, Greater Noida

Contents

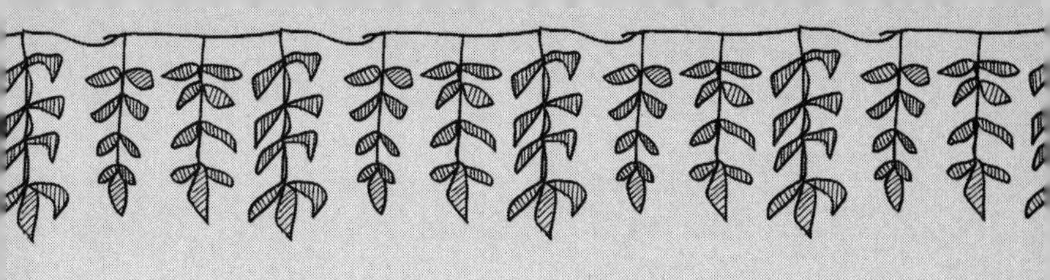

Introduction: Aggregated Truth of Marriages in India

धर्मेच अर्थेच कामेच इमां नातिचरामि।

धर्मेच अर्थेच कामेच इमं नातिचरामि॥

In responsibility, success and pleasure, may I (the bride) always be on your side. In responsibility, success and pleasure, may I (the groom) always be on your side.

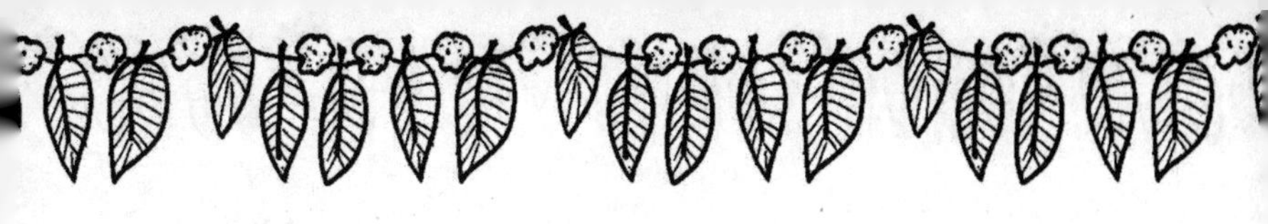

In Hindu temples, gods and goddesses get married. Marriage is as much a divine rite of passage (samskara) as a human one. It marks the union of matter (prakriti) and spirit (purusha). Matter, because it brings in new wealth, status, pleasure, security, and ushers in the next generation, who can inherit the family name and estate. Spirit, because it forces the couple, the family and the community to accommodate new ideas, new emotions, new problems and new solutions. Marriage is described as shubh, mangal, kalyan—full of auspiciousness, goodness and fortune, and not a mere contract. One needs to be vigilant (savadhan) when it happens, as it marks a turning of life, and the world.

But things are not so simple. There are gods and goddesses who do not marry, and their energy is used to kill demons and protect the community. There are gods who marry many goddesses, god-wives who are allowed to find their god-husband in many men, divine couples who fight, separate and then make up. There are gods who choose to dress as mothers, and goddesses who dress like warriors, gods who wear nose-rings and goddesses who sport moustaches, gods who prefer the companionship of men, goddesses who prefer the companionship of women.

Then there are the more practical issues: who can marry whom? There are boundaries created by blood, religion, age, gender, caste, class and whims of fathers and mothers. Who can remarry? How many can you marry? Must you satisfy every spouse? What do you do if the spouse is unsatisfactory? Is fidelity necessary to make a good marriage? Can husbands and wives be happy knowing fully well that the other has many lovers? Can children be raised by single men, single women, groups of women, groups of men? What constitutes a family?

Questions such as these are raised through stories found in Vedas and Puranas: Why is Bhisma, who has no children, considered grandfather by Pandavas and Kauravas? Why is Ganesha married to a banana plant? Why the need to tell stories where celibate Hanuman becomes father of Makaradhwaja? Should the ancestor of the lunar dynasty of kings, Sudyumna-Ila, be called father or mother, husband or wife, for he has both genders? How do you make sense of Oghavati's tale where infidelity is tolerated; and of Jabala's answer about her son's mysterious paternity; and of Kunti's solution when her husband cannot impregnate her?

Hindu wedding rituals contain many aggregated truths from Harappan and Vedic times, to those that came with the Greeks, Sakas, Kushan, Huns, Turks, Afghans, Persians, Arabs, even Europeans. The 'sindoor' and 'bangles' originated in Harappan civilization while the 'mangal sutra' has Dravidian roots. The 'seven-step ritual' comes from Rig Veda, but back then the ritual was for all forms of agreement, not just the wedding union. The 'Kashi-yatra' ritual evokes fears of Brahmins that their sons would become Buddhist or Jain monks. The 'baraat' comes from the Puranic story of Shiva's wild hordes accompanying him to Himavan's house to fetch his bride. The 'sehra' of the horse-riding groom, practised by Muslims also, comes from Central Asian custom of preventing the 'evil eye' from falling upon the handsome young groom as he sets out to fetch his bride. While 'haldi' (turmeric ritual) has Hindu roots, the 'mehendi' (henna ritual) has Islamic roots. The popular 'sangeet ceremony', once a North Indian practice, full of bawdy songs, is now a family song-and-dance affair around the world, thanks to Bollywood. The 'engagement ring' is a Christian idea. The 'wedding certificate', though seemingly secular, has roots in Judeo-Christian-Islamic ideas that value the written over the spoken.

India's ability to aggregate truths comes from its belief in rebirth. No truth was ever replaced, as Indians recognize the need for diverse answers for diverse contexts. There is no concept of absolute truth as in Christianity and Islam. While Abrahamic faiths reject 'false gods', Hinduism does not have such a concept. In Hinduism, all gods are limited (devata) and contribute to the quest for the limitless (bhagavan). God, in Hinduism, is not a judge; he is just an accountant, making sure we always repay our debts accumulated over lifetimes—to our ancestors, our family, our soul, the society, and to nature at large. And the 'dharmik' way of doing that is by establishing a household, says Manusmriti.

This book explores stories around marriage and information that reveal diverse customs and beliefs of mostly, but not entirely, Hindu India. There are brief detours into Buddhist and Jain worlds, and even Muslim communities, for practices found only in India. Special attention is also given to practices now forgotten but alluded to in stories—like a world before marriage was introduced, a world of women without husbands, and a world where spouses (not just women) were abducted.

The sources are Sanskrit, Prakrit, old Tamil literature, the many medieval regional ballads that deal with war and marriage and oral tales including temple lore. I have tried to cover over three thousand years of Indian history and three million square

kilometres of Indian geography.

You may argue with my reading and retelling of the stories. But do engage with them.

Within infinite myths, lies an eternal truth
Who sees it all?
Varuna has but a thousand eyes
Indra, a hundred
You and I, only two

- Jewish, Christian and Muslim weddings introduced the idea of registering the wedding. These religions valued the textual over the oral. Now the world considers registering and documenting marriages a necessary secular practice.
- Jewish patriarchs often had more than one wife.
- Jesus was not married but his presence at a wedding, where he turned water into wine, is seen as proof that he approved of marriage as an institution.
- Muhammad's first wife was older than him, and she was his only wife for 25 years. After her death, he lost the protection granted by her estate and station and was forced to migrate out of Mecca to Medina. He then married 11 women or various political reasons that enabled his triumphant return to Mecca.
- While Christianity viewed sex as Original Sin, Islam saw marriage as gifted by Allah to Adam and Eve.

- The Church, following ancient Roman practice, popularized the idea of monogamy but rejected the Roman practice of divorce.
- Sikhism distinguished itself from Hinduism when it insisted its marriage ritual (Anand Karaj) be governed by a different law.
- Origin of opposition to inter-caste marriage has roots in tribal endogamy seen around the world. As tribal societies crumble, as urbanization and individualism become the norm, marriages are no longer seen as union of clans, but union of individuals.
- Individualism allowed property to be transferred to the Church, and now to the State. Otherwise, property belonged to community, clan or tribe.

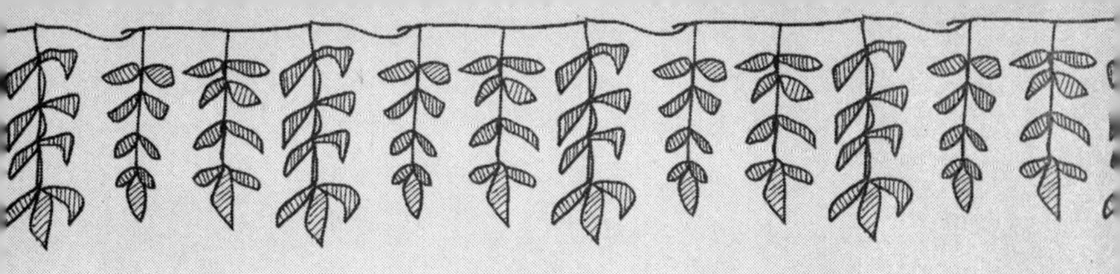

I

Origins

Vedic literature insists that marriage is a rite of passage, without which a man cannot perform a yagna. Without a yagna you cannot feed family, gods or ancestors. What use are you then without marriage?

1. Brahma Chases Shatarupa

What came first? Fire or fuel, desire or flesh, hunger or food. We will never know, for the gods came later. Let it be known that the yagna captures the spirit of desire that propels creation. The altar is the woman and the fire her desire, which seeks the butter poured by the priest. Only then is yagna fruitful.

In the beginning, the first being was lonely, and hungry. He sought companionship and nourishment. And so, he created the first woman.

But the first woman saw the creator as a father, and so his desire for her was considered inappropriate. He tried to grab her; she ran away. She took the form of a cow, a mare, a goose, a doe, and he took the form of a bull, a horse, a gander and a stag. Thus, all male and female creatures came into being. As the mother took many forms she came to be known as Shatarupa. And the father came to be known as Prajapati, who later became Brahma.

From Brahma's mind came many sons. His mind-born son Kashyapa took many wives, and from them were born all kinds of organisms—gods and demons, animals with many limbs (insects), four-limbed with hooves, four-limbed with claws, two-limbed birds and no-limbed reptiles and fish.

Not everyone saw the point of experiencing the world of

senses. Nudged by Narada, they refused to marry and become householders. For that Narada was cursed: he would never get liberation from the world. Those who seek liberation must repay debts to those who help them live—and so they must marry and raise children first. Thus was marriage invented.

- The Vedas have many creation myths. In one, the creator is lonely, and so splits himself to create the diverse universe. This story is elaborated in later texts such as Puranas. Vedas are over 3000 years old while Puranas are less than 2000 years old.
- In Brahmanas (late Vedic scriptures) diversity is created when Prajapati chases his daughter who takes the form of various animals. In Puranas, Brahma's mind-born son Marichi has a son called Kashyapa who marries many women and produces nature's diversity. The common father explains why all creatures have the same spirit (atma) and why we say 'the whole world is one family' (vasudhaiva kutumbakam) but the fact about different mothers explains the different kinds of species, bodies and communities.
- The curse of Narada found in many Puranas captures the tension between Puranic Hinduism that valued marriage and householder's life and opposed the monastic life, i.e., Buddhism and Jainism.
- Hindu monks became a dominant force in Hindu society only after the waning of Buddhism, and the rise of Nath-jogis, Adi Shankara's Advaita and Bhakti movement.

2. Sati Chooses Shiva

Daksha's youngest daughter decided to marry Shiva, the hermit, who lived a solitary existence in the snow-clad Himalayas. Daksha disapproved. Shiva hated desire. He had long ago shot the arrow that had prevented Prajapati from chasing Shatarupa. He would not be a good husband, or a worthy son-in-law.

But Sati was adamant. She left her father's house, went to Shiva's abode and becomes his wife. Only he did not know what it meant to be a husband

An angry Daksha invited all his sons-in-law to his house but not Shiva. When Sati demanded an explanation, he insulted Shiva so terribly that Sati decided to kill herself in her father's fire altar.

When Shiva heard this, he exploded in a terrifying temper and transformed into Virabhadra and beheaded Daksha. He then wandered the earth carrying the corpse of his beloved Sati, clinging to it until it fell piece by piece across the earth. Thus, the hermit, who desired nothing, discovered heartbreak.

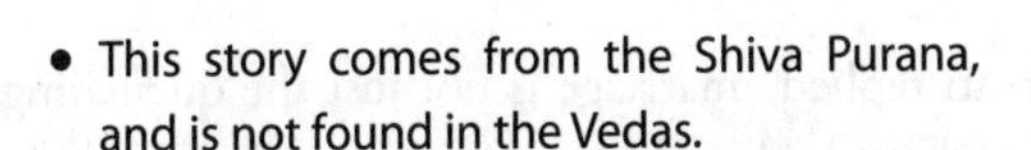

- This story comes from the Shiva Purana, and is not found in the Vedas.
- It reveals the tension between Daksha who favours the yagna (outer fire such as the hearth, funeral pyre, sacrificial altar), hence the household; and Shiva who favours tapasya (inner fire of meditation and contemplation), hence the single life.

- Sati chooses her husband. She refuses to be offered to the gods, like her other sisters. This is an acknowledgement of female agency, of self-choice (svayamvar).
- Here, the tension between father-in-law and son-in-law draws attention to the need that marriage is not about two individuals but about two families. The failure of Sati's marriage is compensated when she is reborn as Parvati.

3. Shiva Becomes a Groom for Parvati

Shiva said that he had no need for a wife. He isolated himself in the snow-clad mountains. The gods, who wanted Shiva to father a child, who would lead them into victorious battles, sent Kama, the god of desire, to enchant him. Shiva opened his third eye and destroyed Kama.

Parvati, the mountain princess, meditated and thought of none but Shiva, until Shiva appeared and offered her a boon.

'Marry me,' she said.

But he told her that he had conquered Kama. Why did he need a wife then?

'Because,' Parvati replied, 'marriage is not just the quenching of desire. It is also about looking beyond one's own desires at the desires of others. It is about caring and sharing.' Shiva liked her words and agreed to marry her.

In her last life as Sati, Parvati had left her father's house to be with Shiva. This time, she asked Shiva to come to fetch her from her father's house. He agreed. Only, he did not know how to be a groom. He did not know how to present himself, suitably adorned. He had no relatives, or gifts to give.

Shiva arrived at Parvati's house seated on a bull, covered with ash, hair matted, snakes around his neck. His relatives were denizens of crematoriums, ghosts and goblins. His gift was a string of skulls, and a pot of poison. Parvati's mother, Mena, refused to accept this man as her son-in-law.

Parvati begged Shiva to let Daksha's sons-in-law, the gods, to adorn him. They bathed him and anointed him with sandal paste and bedecked him with flowers. Shiva was thus transformed, by a wedding, from a wild hermit to a refined householder.

- This story comes from the Shiva Purana and establishes the wedding ritual of the groom coming to claim the wife.
- It is a story of a groom being domesticated: the hermit being made a householder; the barbarians being shown what is civilized conduct.
- The unruly behaviour of men in a baraat are said to be reminders of Shiva's ganas, who are domesticated by the bride's household. Shiva's 'baraat' is a phrase to refer to a troop of unruly men.
- As horse riding became popular in Rajput lands, the groom was expected to come to the bride's house dressed as a king; on a mare with a sword. Many folk hero gods ride mares who are goddesses protecting them. However, many

non-land-owning communities were prohibited to ride the mare. Thus, was caste hierarchy established in India. Even today we hear of grooms from dalit communities being abused and even attacked for riding mares on their wedding.

4. Lakshmi Chooses Vishnu

We call them gods and demons, but they are actually devas and asuras who live in the sky and under the earth. Both are sons of Kashyapa by different mothers, Aditi and Diti. Devas and asuras hated each other.

The gods decided to churn out Lakshmi, the goddess of fortune, who had dissolved herself in the ocean of milk. They decided to use Meru, the king of mountains, as the churning spindle and Vasuki, the king of snakes, as the churning rope. Vishnu took the form of a turtle and held up the churn, keeping it afloat.

The devas did not have enough force to operate the churn themselves. Vishnu told them to take help from asuras. The asuras agreed and pulled the tail of the serpent while devas pulled the neck. But they pulled simultaneously, like a tug-of-war, as if they were used to competing.

Vishnu told them that to churn, they had to collaborate, pull alternatively, in rhythmic regularity. Devas had to pull while the asuras paused, and asuras had

to pull when the devas paused. They had to pull just enough for the rope to not unwound itself. Thus, the churning began, and it was successful.

Great treasures came with it. Political power embodied in horses, elephants, bows and conch shells. Economic power embodied in trees, and cows and gems. Pleasure in the form of singers and musicians and dancers and wine. Poison came too, that Shiva consumed and held in his throat.

The devas took all this and refused to share it with the asuras and drove them back to the subterranean regions. The asuras swore they would keep attacking the realm of the devas, giving them not a moment's peace to enjoy their fortune.

Finally, Lakshmi arose, seated on a lotus. Indra, king of devas, thought she would choose him as husband, for he had all the political and economic powers of the world, and every form of pleasure fathomable. But Lakshmi chose Vishnu because Indra had helped no one and cared only for his own pleasure.

- This story comes from the Vishnu Purana.
- During Hindu wedding ceremony, the story of the churning of ocean is often chanted to remind the couple how their marriage is a churning to produce the treasures from the ocean of milk.
- The story draws attention to the tension between conflict and collaboration. Indra thrives in conflict and is rejected by Lakshmi, goddess of fortune, who prefers collaboration.

5. Varaha Rescues Bhoo-devi

Hiranyaksha decided to claim the earth as his own. So, he grabbed the earth-goddess and dragged her with him under the sea. Bhoo-devi cried out and Brahma heard her cries. From his nostrils emerged a boar that dived into the sea, gored Hiranyaksha to death and raised Bhoo-devi on his snout back to the surface of the sea.

Bhoo-devi recognized the boar as Vishnu; she declared that he was her husband, her protector and lord of earth, Bhupati. She embraced him and from their passionate embrace all mountains and valleys came into being. He plunged his tusks into the earth and made it fertile with all kinds of plants.

- This story comes from the Vishnu Purana.
- Here the man's role as protector and defender of his wife is established.
- In many mythologies, Vedas refer to the earth (Prithvi) as mother and the sky (Dyaus) as the father. Over time, Prithvi became Bhoo-devi and Dyaus became Vishnu, blue as the sky, who watches over her and protects her.

6. Lakshmi Soothes Narasimha

Hiranakashipu had secured a boon by which he could not be killed by a man or an animal, at day or at night, inside or outside a dwelling, neither on earth nor in the sky, with neither a weapon nor a tool. This made him invincible and rather intolerable. The over-smart asura thought he had outsmarted death itself until Vishnu took the form of Narasimha, half-man and half-lion, and tore his gut out, at twilight (neither day nor night), at the threshold (neither inside nor outside), on his lap (neither sky nor earth) with his bare claws (neither weapon nor tool).

But when Narasimha drank the blood of the asura, he was consumed by rage, passion and madness. The gods did not know how to control him. Shiva tried to control him using force but that worked only temporarily. So, the gods told Lakshmi to intervene. She came to him with a smile on her face, speaking soothing words. Gently, she calmed him down, sat in his lap and reminded him who he was, a god who cares. That is what spouses do.

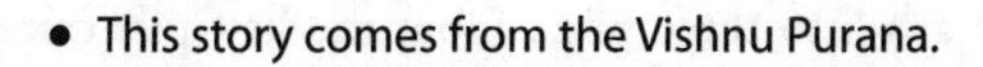

- This story comes from the Vishnu Purana.
- Images of Lakshmi-Narasimha are worshipped in Andhra Pradesh. Narasimha is considered to be ferocious (ugra) to be worshipped alone and so is accompanied by the wife. This makes his form auspicious (shubh). Without her, he is not enshrined in a temple.

- Similarly, fierce forms of Shiva, like Rudra, are always balanced by the loving image of Gauri. When the goddess becomes wild as Kali, Shiva takes the form of Shankara, lies in her path and calms her down with his tranquil beauty.
- The story draws attention to the role of spouses in balancing the energies of their husbands or wives. Like the Chinese yin-yang, Indian tantra has ida-pingala, or moon-sun, to represent the balanced couple.

7. Gangamma's Desire

Adi-Para-Shakti, the primal mother, known popularly as Gangamma, was lonely and so she created Brahma. On his birth, Brahma addressed her as Amma, mother. So, she could not marry him. Then she created Vishnu. On his birth, Vishnu addressed her as Akka, sister. So, she could not marry him. Finally, she created Shiva, who did not say anything. She liked him and asked him to marry her.

'But you have three eyes,' he said, 'and I, only two.' So, she gave him her third eye. But he did not know how to control this third eye. It produced fire and turned Gangamma into a heap of ash. Shiva divided the ash into three piles. From the first pile came Saraswati who married Brahma. From the second pile came Lakshmi who married Vishnu and from the third pile came Kali who married Shiva.

But not all ash was used. From the remainder ash came 84,000 village goddesses (grama-devi) who belong to everyone but are owned by no one. Each one is a mother without a husband. Each

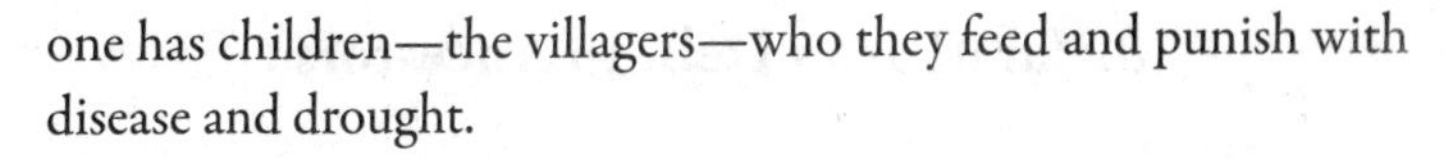

one has children—the villagers—who they feed and punish with disease and drought.

- This story comes from folk and village traditions (desi parampara). It's an oral tradition. It gives primacy to women's desire.
- Vedas do not refer to the goddess but beyond the restricted domain of Vedas was the Indian village where she has always played a major role.
- The annual sacrifice of goats and buffaloes to the village goddess is a reminder of her desires and is ritually connected with marriage. Like the sword carried by the groom in Rajput weddings, we see sex and violence being ritually inter-mingled.
- Marriage is considered both sexual (establishment of home, with kitchen, bedroom, courtyard and entrance pavilion) and violent (end of independence).
- The union of three Hindu gods (Brahma, Vishnu, Shiva) and three Hindu goddesses (Saraswati, Lakshmi, Durga) is a later Puranic invention to create symmetry and to highlight the importance of marriage in the divine realm. Historically speaking, the goddesses had independent origins. Earliest images of Lakshmi come from Buddhist art, and earliest images of Saraswati come from Jain art. Durga appears in Kushan art for the first time, killing the buffalo.

8. Jaratkaru's Debt to Ancestors

Jaratkaru was not interested in the yagna that binds a man to society. He wanted to do tapasya, break free from culture, and nature. But then his ancestors appeared before him in a vision, hanging upside down over a dark abyss called Put—the hell reserved for people whose sons do not father children.

Repay your debt, begged the ancestors (pitr). Only then could they hope to be reborn. They wanted their son (putra) to produce a son (putra) to save them from the hell called Put. When the son produces children, and their children produce children, the dead can return to the land of the living. Those who experienced re-death (punar-mrityu) will experience re-birth (punar-janma).

So Jaratkaru decided to get married. He was a reluctant groom. His first condition was that he would marry a woman who shared his name. The ancestors ensured that he met Mansa, sister of the snake-king, Vasuki, who was also called Jaratkaru. He married her and made her pregnant.

His second condition was that she should never disturb him. One day, he was sleeping, when it was time to make the evening offering to the gods. She woke him up and he got so angry that he left her, leaving her to raise their child on her own. But, at least, he had repaid his debt to the ancestors, and so would no more be tormented by them.

The son of this union of Jaratkaru and Jaratkaru was Astika, half man and half snake. He stopped the terrible snake sacrifice of Janamejaya, reminding the king of the long association of humans and snakes. Thus, the son of Jaratkaru saved the world, just as by fathering him Jaratkaru saved his ancestors from the hell called Put.

A wife enables a man to repay his debt to his ancestors, by

fathering children. That is why marriage was invented. A wife thus liberates her husband from debt. She saves the ancestors from eternal suffering.

When father's name and lineage determined social status then marriage became essential.

- This story comes from the Mahabharata.
- In the Bengali Mansa Mangal, the husband, Jaratkaru, leaves his wife, Mansa, because she is tricked by her step-mother, Chandi, to adorn herself with snakes.
- Hindu men perform the 'shraadh' ritual to feed ancestors (pitr) and to promise that they will produce children (putr) to liberate the dead from the land of the dead by enabling rebirth in the land of the living.
- Here, the man's role in raising the child is completely ignored.

9. Father of Jabala's Son

A boy went to Gautama and asked to be a student.
'Who is your father?' asked the teacher.
The boy replied, 'My mother said she does not know who my father is. The men who came to her never told her their name. My mother's name is Jabala and everyone calls me Jabali, her son.'

Impressed by the boy's honesty, Gautama gave

Jabali another name: Satyakama, one who seeks the truth, for he was indeed the seeker of truth, one who is unafraid of the truth.

- This story comes from the Upanishads.
- The spiritually evolved person does not care for lineage. Lineage matters in the material world where status is determined by property and property is passed on to legitimate children.
- Until marriage laws became universal, children were identified through their mothers. Hence Pandavas (sons of King Pandu) but also referred to as Kauntaneya (sons of Kunti) and Madreya (sons of Madri).
- Many Hindu clans trace their origin to a Kula-devi, who was probably the primal matriarch. The Kula-deva is merely guardian, not father.

10. Shvetaketu Code

Udalaka's son, Shvetaketu, found his mother in the arms of another man. Horrified, he complained to his father who said a woman is free to do as she pleases. 'How then do I know that you are my father? Am I the fruit of your seed?'

To this, Udalaka said that fatherhood is more of an emotional fact, rather than a biological one. But this did not please Shvetaketu who put together the laws of marriage by which a woman should be faithful to the husband. She could only sleep with another man, for the purpose of having children, if her husband could not father children on his own, and if her husband granted her permission.

- This story comes from the Mahabharata.
- This story firmly establishes relationship of marriage to determining paternity of the child. This was not necessary before, where marriage was about partnership not necessarily children.
- Jain traditions state that when the world was young, couples emerged from the same womb and so were also brothers and sisters. They produced children without sex, or contact, merely by thought. Sexual act produced contamination and sex became prevalent only much later after which the wheel of time turned and the world became old, decayed and corrupt.

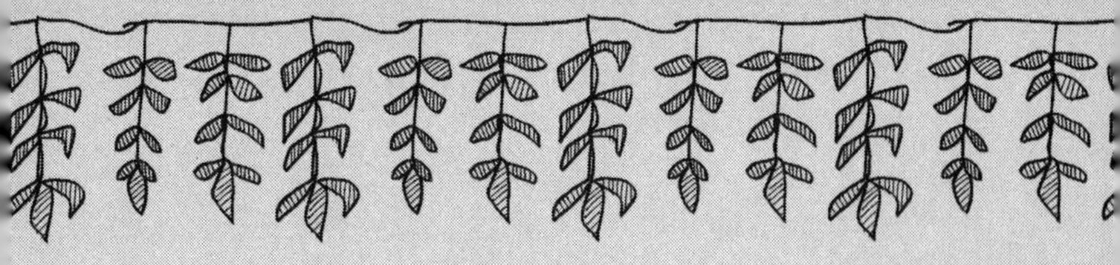

II

Singledom

Buddha and Tirthankaras are venerated as they walk away from marriage in search of higher truths. But Brahma curses Narada as he is against marriage, household and children. Then we learn of Hanuman and Nath-jogis who have magical power, even immortality, owing to ascetic practices. Gandharvas and Apsaras are not expected to marry. Courtesans are not allowed to marry. Widows are not allowed to remarry. Marriage certainly is not universal.

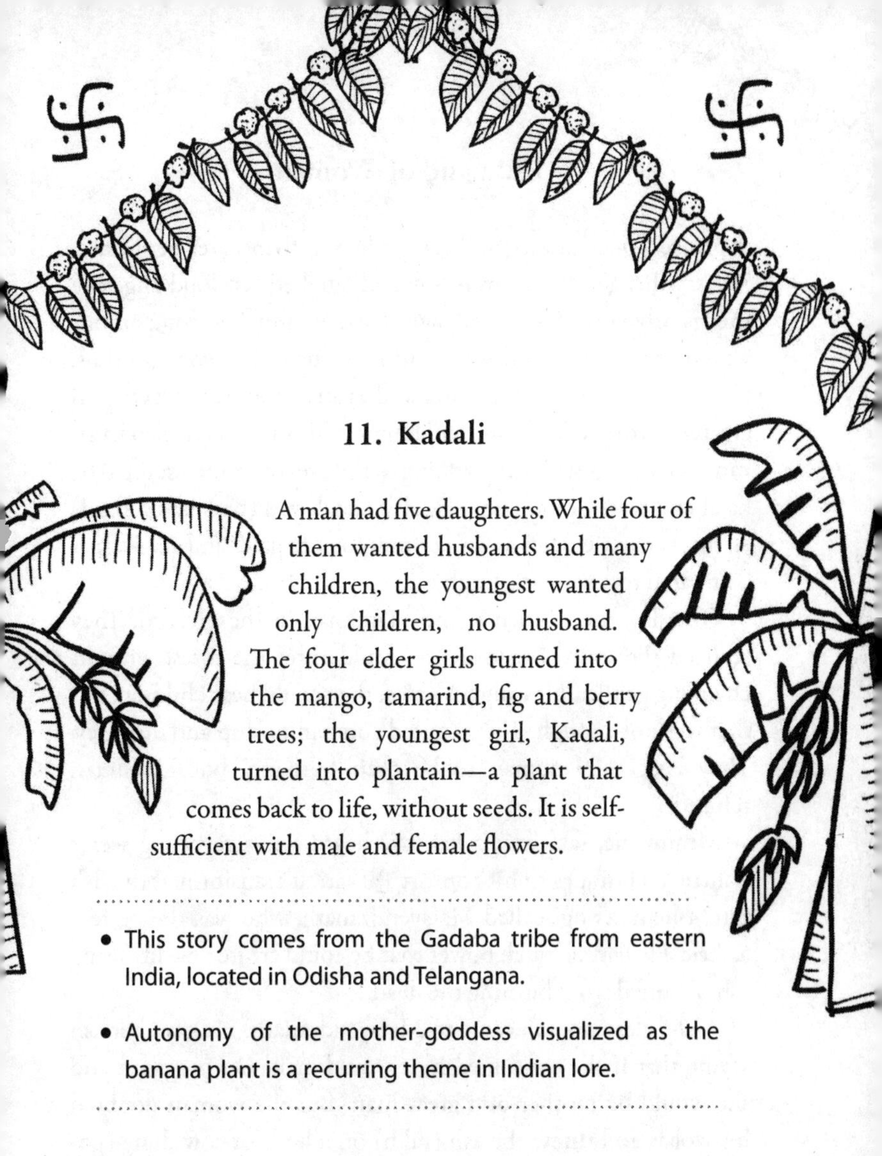

11. Kadali

A man had five daughters. While four of them wanted husbands and many children, the youngest wanted only children, no husband. The four elder girls turned into the mango, tamarind, fig and berry trees; the youngest girl, Kadali, turned into plantain—a plant that comes back to life, without seeds. It is self-sufficient with male and female flowers.

- This story comes from the Gadaba tribe from eastern India, located in Odisha and Telangana.
- Autonomy of the mother-goddess visualized as the banana plant is a recurring theme in Indian lore.

12. Land of Women

A princess once saw a gandharva as he was flying over her palace. She saw his genitals from below and laughed out loud angering the gandharva who cursed her that she and her companions would live in this land where all men turn into women. Thus, he deprived them of romantic and erotic pleasures forever and created a world of yearning and longing. This world is called kajri-van (cloudy forest), kajri referring to the eyes of women stained by kajal and tears of longing. It is also kadali-van (banana-orchard) as the banana is seen as an autonomous female, and its stem is compared to a woman's thigh.

One day, the women found Hanuman in the orchard. They realized that only a true ascetic could enter the forest without changing gender. Hearing his voice, they could bear children, but that was not enough. They wanted companionship and intimacy. They begged Hanuman to be their husband, but Hanuman refused.

Meanwhile, far away, a fish overheard Shiva revealing secret Tantric techniques to his consort Parvati. It transformed the fish into a man, a yogi called Matsyendranath, who was the perfect ascetic. He had so much power that he could create new life using ash obtained from burning the dead.

A childless woman came to Matsyendranath. He gave her ash saying that if she consumed it, it would make her pregnant and she would be mother of a great man. But the woman doubted his words and threw the ash (rakh) on a heap of cow dung (go-bar). A child emerged from the heap. Matsyendranath called him Gorakhnath, his son and student.

One day, Matsyendranath went missing and Gorakhnath

realized he had entered the kajri-van and been enchanted by the women there. They were known as yoginis who derived their power by enchanting men. His guru was a yogi, who derived his power by staying away from women. As a perfect ascetic, Matsyendranath had not turned into a woman, much to the yoginis' delight, but he had clearly lost his mind and so could not escape. To save him, Gorakhnath entered the banana orchard.

Kajri-van could not turn Gorakhnath into a woman as he was a perfect ascetic himself. But he disguised himself in female attire to avoid the lustful gaze of the resident women. He played a drum and sang a song reminding his guru of his life before the enchantment, and of how the world of women and lust leads to mortality, and how rejecting women, lust and household creates immortality.

- The yogi becomes jogi in folk literature. But he is not a mere ascetic seeking higher truths; he is also a siddha, with magical powers. He is supremely attractive, can make infertile lands fertile and give children to childless women, without touching them. His greatest enemy is the yogini or jogini, visualized as sexually deprived women, who get powers by seducing young virile men (jawans).

- Nath-jogi literature emerged in the tenth century and remains an oral tradition. It speaks of monastic men and lustful women, jogis and joginis, and the tension between them. We learn of Puran-Bhagat, whose stepmother accuses him of rape when he rejects her advances and so his father cuts his four limbs. Gorakhnath restores his limbs, and he becomes renowned as Chauranginath (four-limbed ascetic). Gopichand very reluctantly gives up his many wives and lovers to become a jogi by the grace of Jalandarnath so that he does not die. Rani Sundari immolates herself when she hears the lie that the handsome jogi (Rasalu in disguise) she desires has been killed by her jealous lover.

- The jogis were probably wandering peasant-warriors determined to be faithful to wives back home, who sang songs like baramasa (twelve months of separation).
- Hanuman's celibacy makes his body so strong and potent that a drop of his sweat makes a fish pregnant. She bears his son, Makaradhvaja. Such stories are told to establish the virility of single gods as many argue that the god is single because he isn't potent.
- Many researchers feel that Buddha was perhaps not married. Stories of his marriage and son came later to establish his virility. In Jain tradition, there are some who believe Mahavir was married and had a daughter; others who insist he was never married.

13. Manimekalai

Manimekalai's mother, Madhavi, was a courtesan and so was her grandmother, Chitra. While the grandmother was at peace with her courtesan life and wanted her children and grandchildren to follow her path, the mother wanted to marry Kovalan, who was married to Kannagi.

When Kovalan became poor, having spent all his wealth on Madhavi, Madhavi was told to abandon him and find a new lover. She did as she was told, and a heartbroken Kovalan returned to his wife, and migrated to the city of Madurai, where he was wrongly accused of theft and killed without a proper hearing by the king. News of his death broke Madhavi's heart. Manimekalai, daughter of Madhavi and Kovalan, became an orphan as a result.

Manimekalai was raised to be a courtesan by her grandmother. But she was confused. The Chola prince Udaya desired her and wanted to marry her. He pursued her everywhere but Manimekalai rejected his advances. She desired him, but desired freedom from suffering even more. She was protected by many Buddhist nuns and goddesses, who also taught her the Buddhist doctrine. They told her that in her last life she was married to Udaya: she had been kind to Buddhist monks while he had been rude. And so, in this life she had the fortune of becoming a nun and he would suffer heartbreak.

To protect Manimekalai, a goddess gave her the face of a yakshini. When the yakshini's husband saw her, he approached her as a man approaches his wife. But Manimekalai-with-the-yakshi-face frowned. When she saw prince Udaya, she smiled with her yakshi face. The yaksha was confused: why was his wife frowning on seeing him and smiling on seeing Udaya. Suspecting that his wife was having an affair with Udaya, he killed Udaya in a fit of jealousy. Manimekalai burst into tears, and her original face was restored. The yaksha ran away and everyone blamed Manimekalai for the murder. The goddesses and the nuns came to her defence.

Observing the pain caused by passion, Manimekalai was freed of all doubts and decided to walk the Buddhist path as a nun. She sought food as alms not just for herself but also the poor and needy. She travelled to other lands where she spread the word of the Buddha.

- Manimekalai's story comes from Tamil Buddhist lore, roughly 1400 years ago, before the rise of Bhakti. It refers to Hindu lore, and Jain lore, and marks the transition from old Buddhism that was highly individualistic to the later Buddhism where deities help the followers of Buddhism.
- Manimekalai refers to many Buddhist goddesses who help nuns.
- The Mahabharata tells us the story of a nun called Shandili who wanted to stay celibate. Garuda, the bird, flying overhead desired her and instantly lost the power over his wings. He fell down and regained power of flight only after he apologized to Shandili.
- The Mahabharata tells us the story of a nun called Sulabha who teaches Janaka that soul is not gendered and that he

must focus on the soul than the gender of the biological body.

- The idea of a chaste woman being able to protect herself is a recurring theme in Hindu lore, which has the unfortunate sequence of people assuming that women who get molested and sexually abused are unchaste.

- Buddha allowed women to become nuns after much hesitation as he, like many, believed women have greater sexual desire than men. There are more Buddhist laws for nuns than for monks. Jainism also has monastic orders for women.

- Tantric monastic practices believe that semen is necessary for attaining moksha, freedom from cycle of rebirths. Women therefore have to be chaste so that they can be reborn as men in the next life, before they can hope to attain moksha.

14. Karaikal Ammaiyar

Punidavati lived in the village of Karaikal with her husband Paramadatta, a seafaring merchant. She was so devoted to Shiva that the lord bestowed upon her magical powers. Her ability to conjure sweet mangoes by merely wishing for them, scared her husband who, after his next voyage, did not return home. Instead, he went to the city of Madurai, married another woman and raised a family with her.

When Punidavati learnt why her husband had left her, she realized she had no more use of her beautiful body. By the grace of Shiva, she transformed herself into a crone, with shrivelled breasts and gaunt features so that no man could look upon her with eyes of desire. Thus, she was free to devote herself to her lord. She became renowned as Karaikal Ammaiyar, the matriarch of Karaikal.

- Karaikal Ammaiyar is a Nayamnar and her story is told in the Tamil Periya Puranam.
- Bhakti, or passionate devotion to a single god, became a major theme of Hinduism about 1000 years ago. It not only rejected the sterility of monasticism but also rejected the tensions involved in households.
- The songs composed by women often reveal their desire to be loved for who they were. They were seeking ideal love that no mortal man seemed to be able to provide. Hence, their longing for god, attributing to him the qualities of the perfect beloved.
- The songs composed by men visualize themselves as women yearning for their lover, who happens to be God.

15. Kundalakesi

A rich merchant's daughter named Kundalakesi once saw a criminal being taken for execution. She fell in love with him and begged her father to secure his hand in marriage. The merchant could never say no to his daughter and so used his wealth to get the criminal released. Kundalakesi thus got the husband she wanted.

But as the years passed, the love waned. The couple kept fighting and irritating each other. Kundalakesi kept mocking her husband for his criminal past. Angry, he tried to kill her, but she managed to kill him instead.

She then became a nun and found peace in the words of Buddha, that desire is the cause of suffering.

- This story comes from Tamil Buddhist traditions.
- The story draws attention to a woman's desire and her father's indulgence of that desire. The girl gets her way.

16. Kunigarga's Daughter

The daughter of sage Kunigarga performed austerities and refused any contact with men. She wanted liberation. But though she conquered her senses, she was not allowed to enter heaven as she had not performed her worldly duties.

When she returned to earth, no man would marry her as she was old and ugly. So, she offered half the merits of her austerities to any man who would marry her. The young sage Shringavan accepted her offer, married her and made love to her for one night.

The next day, she abandoned her youthful body and discovered she could enter heaven, alone. Shringavan also gave up all his wealth, even his property and propitiated the gods till he could rise up into heaven, after her.

- This story comes from the Mahabharata and is told to Balarama when he reaches a pilgrimage site (tirtha).
- Kunigarga's daughter is called vriddha-kanya, or old maid, and deals with the problem of a nun, or monk, not fulfilling her biological obligation. Both are expected to have sexual experience, and maybe produce a child, before renouncing the world. Thus, marriage is mandatory even for renunciants.
- The story says that the young man agreed to marry the old woman in order to gain spiritual merit that he uses to get himself to heaven. The idea of a younger man finding an older woman attractive is resisted by storytellers.
- Many girls worship Shiva on Mondays to get good husbands.
- Married women worship Shiva and Parvati in festivals like Gangaur and Teej especially in Rajasthan.

17. Amba

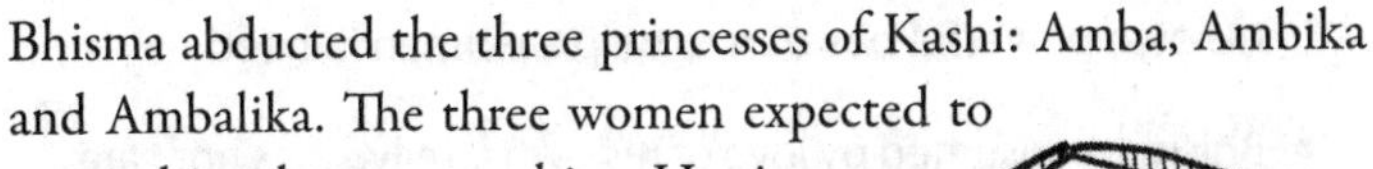

Bhisma abducted the three princesses of Kashi: Amba, Ambika and Ambalika. The three women expected to marry him, but on reaching Hastinapur learnt that he had given up his conjugal rights so that his old father could marry the fisherwoman, Satyavati.

Satyavati's children were weak. The first, Chitra, died young and the second, Vichitra, could not get a wife by himself. So, the abducted princesses had to marry Vichitra.

Amba told Vichitra that she was in love with Shalva and wanted to be with the man of her choice. Vichitra let her go. But Shalva refused to accept Amba as she had been tainted, already claimed by Bhisma.

Amba returned to Hastintapur. This time, Vichitra refused to accept her, as she had become a gift he had already given away. 'Who will be my husband?' she asked. She blamed Bhisma for her misfortune and begged him to marry her to make amends. Bhisma refused.

Amba wandered the earth, determined to be the cause of Bhisma's death, because he had ruined her marriage.

- This story comes from the Mahabharata and shows how patriarchy works, and how a woman is seen as being contaminated by another man's touch.

- The weak younger brother takes advantage of his elder brother's strength to get him a wife. But he does not use his own powerful position to help a woman in need.
- Bhisma, consumed by love of his own family, does not care for Amba, and that indifference is seen as adharma and eventually becomes the cause of his death.

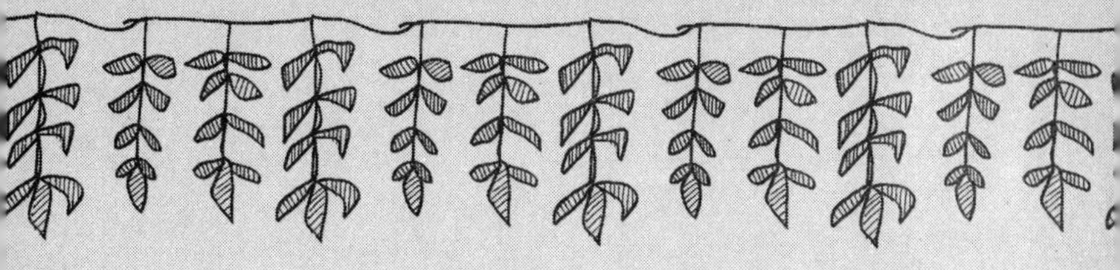

III

Wooing

How do you get a groom or a bride? Do you woo, abduct or buy? Does consent matter? All possibilities exist, but within boundaries, as indicated by the ever present 'roti-and-beti' (bread-and-daughter) rule, which allows marriage only within communities that once followed the same vocation. Thus is jati (caste) established.

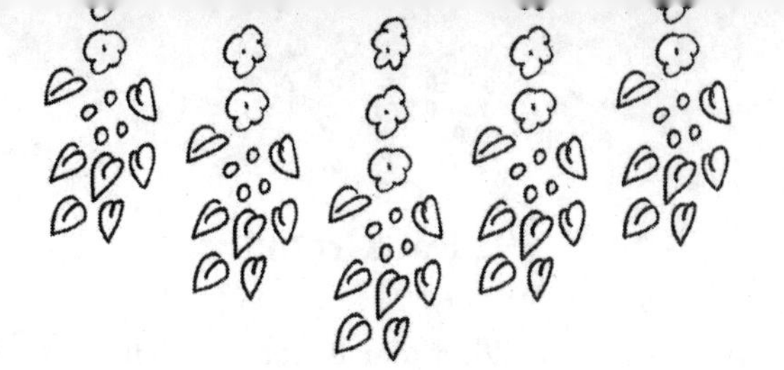

18. Apala

Apala could not find a husband as she had a skin disease. She wandered without a husband aimlessly in the mountains until she accidentally came upon the shoots of the soma plant and began chewing it. As the juice emerged between her teeth, Indra appeared and asked her to give him his favourite drink, soma. Apala gave the drink and a pleased Indra offered her boon.

Make me beautiful so that I can get a husband, she said. So, Indra drew her through the eye of one of his chariot wheels. She shed her diseased skin and began to glow. Thus, she found a husband.

- This story comes from the Rig Veda. The importance of beauty is asserted in this story.
- In later Sanskrit literature, such as *Kathasaritsagar*, we come upon stories where kings are not allowed to marry beautiful women like Unmada, due to the fear that they will use their beauty (kama) to distract the king from royal duty (dharma).

19. Rat-Groom

While praying for a child, a female baby rat fell in front of a childless couple, having slipped from the talons of a falcon. The couple saw this as a divine answer. So, using their magic powers they turned the baby rat into a human girl-child and raised her with love. When it was time for marriage, the girl wanted to marry the strongest being in the world.

'The sun?' asked the father.

'The cloud covers his face,' replied the daughter.

'The cloud?' asked the father.

'The mountain blocks its path,' replied the daughter.

'The mountain?'

'No, the rat bores holes in it.'

'Who then?' asked the father.

'The rat, of course,' said the daughter.

The couple smiled and restored their daughter to her original form and got her married to a rat.

- This story comes from the Panchatantra and is meant to give a lesson that nature is more important than nurture: you cannot train a rat to think like a human.
- The story explains caste endogamy that people prefer to marry within their own ilk.
- Brahmins who wrote the dharma-shastra around the same time that Panchatantra was compiled were obsessed with

endogamy. They classified society into four groups (varna): brahmin, kshatriya, vaishya, shudra. They insisted that marriage has to take place within the varna and forbade mixed marriages, especially if the man was from lower caste. Stories such as these reinforced that idea.

20. Gunakeshi and Sumukha

Indra's charioteer Matali had a daughter called Gunakeshi who fell in love with Sumukha, a Naga. But the marriage was not possible as Garuda, the mighty eagle, threatened to eat Sumukha if he stepped out of the nether world.

Gunakeshi begged Indra for help but Garuda was too strong for him. So, Indra sought the help of Vishnu who told Garuda to leave Sumukha alone. When Garuda argued that snakes are his natural food, Vishnu placed his hand on his wings and thus pinned him to the ground, preventing him from flying, until he agreed to let Sumukha emerge from Naga-loka and rise towards the celestial regions to marry Gunakeshi.

- This story is from the Mahabharata.
- This story shows how god intervenes to enable a girl to marry her beloved man. She belongs to the sky and he belongs to the earth. Opposition comes from the bird who flies in the sky and eats snakes. Is this a metaphor for family opposition to love marriages?
- Similar tales are found in Buddhist literature, of a man asking Garuda to eat him instead of a naga-youth who is supposed to marry. Garuda feels horrible and lets the man and the naga-youth go.

21. Mandodari Marries Ravana

Parvati wanted Shiva to build a home. But Shiva did not understand the concept of a home. She said, 'I need a place that keeps me warm in winter.'

He suggested they go to the crematorium.

She said, 'I need a place that keeps me cold in summer.'

He suggested they go to Mount Kailash covered with snow.

She said, 'I need a place that keeps me dry in rains.'

He suggested they live in caves. Frustrated, she ordered Shiva to build her a palace. Shiva did not know how.

Shiva asked his devotee, Ravana, to help. Being a Vedic scholar, well-versed in architecture, he built Shiva a palace. It was beautiful and it made Parvati very happy. Pleased that his wife was pleased, Shiva offered Ravana a gift. And Ravana, greedy as ever, said

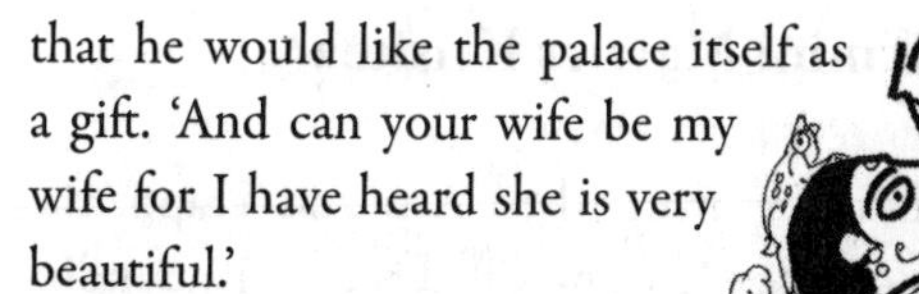

that he would like the palace itself as a gift. 'And can your wife be my wife for I have heard she is very beautiful.'

Shiva, the one who is without guile, said, 'So be it.' He did not understand the concept of marriage.

Parvati divined how Ravana was taking advantage of Shiva's innocence. To teach him a lesson she took a frog (manduka) and turned the frog into a replica of herself. Ravana saw this duplicate Parvati and took her to Lanka in his new palace. She called herself Mandodari, as she was actually a frog, but pompous Ravana never realized he had been tricked by the Goddess.

- The story of Parvati's house is from Marathi folklore and the story of Mandodari is from Telugu folklore.
- Shiva is visualized as Bholenath, the guileless ascetic, who does not understand the concept of property or wife. He does not understand the concept of 'mine', which is why he owns nothing, neither wife, nor family, neither clothes nor property.
- Ravana is smart and takes advantage of Shiva's naiveté but Shakti teaches him a lesson. What does not matter to Shiva, matters to Shakti.

22. Rukmini Marries Krishna

Kansa, king of Mathura, was married to Asti and Prapti, the daughters of Jarasandha. When Krishna killed Kansa, Jarasandha swore to destroy Krishna and ended up burning the city of Mathura. He assumed the fire claimed Krishna's life, but Krishna managed to escape and set up home far away in the west on an island called Dwarka.

Jarasandha wanted Shishupala, king of Chedi, to marry Rukmini, the princess of Vidarbha. But Rukmini did not want Shishupala as husband. She wanted to marry Krishna. She was convinced he had survived the burning of Mathura. She begged a wandering minstrel to travel across the known world, find Krishna and give her message to him.

On the day, she was to marry Shishupala, a chariot appeared in the horizon, and whisked her away. It was Krishna! Her brother, Rukmi, chased this chariot to bring her back but Krishna defeated him in a duel and took Rukmini to Dwarka to be his queen.

Years later, Rukmini's son Pradyumna was given in marriage

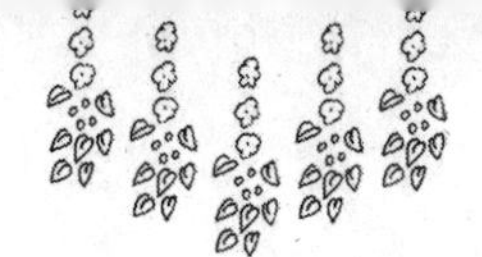

to Rukmi's daughter, Rukmavati. In that wedding, during the celebrations, Rukmi played the game of dice with Krishna's brother, Balarama. He cheated and an angry Balarama clubbed him to death.

- This story comes from Bhagavata Purana.
- This is a combination of Rakshasa-vivah (abduction of bride) and Gandharva-vivah (love and mutual consent).
- In many tribal communities, brides are chosen through rituals of hide-and-seek and mock abduction.

23. Satyabhama's Syamantaka

The Yadavas descended from Yadu, whose father Yayati had cursed him that his descendants would never be kings. So Yadavas were not a monarchy; they were an oligarchy, with many chiefs. One of the chiefs was Surasena. His grandson, Krishna, was raised by cowherds, to protect him from his uncle, Kansa, Ugrasena's son, who had declared himself king of Yadavas. The boy eventually returned, killed his uncle, and reestablished the Yadava oligarchy. As he was raised by cowherds, Krishna was seen as lacking in refinement; someone considered as an unworthy groom.

Surajit was another Yadava nobleman who

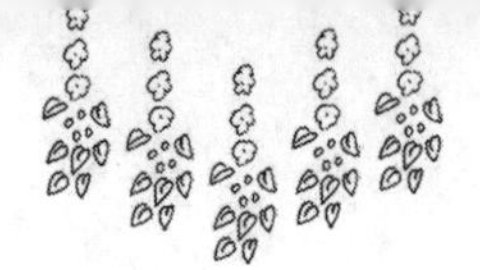

had a jewel given to him by Surya, the sun-god, called Syamantaka, that brought him great luck. Krishna told Surajit that the jewel should belong to all Yadavas rather than him alone to ensure prosperity for the community. Surajit refused.

A few days later, Surajit's brother, Prasenajit, was found dead in the forest. The Syamantaka gem he wore around his neck had gone missing. Everyone blamed Krishna, known to steal clothes of milkmaids.

Krishna investigated and found footprints of a lion near Prasenajit's corpse and footprints of a bear a little ahead. Krishna realized Prasenajit had been killed by a lion who had been killed by a bear who had probably taken the jewel. He followed the clues and came to the cave where a bear was playing with the jewel. Krishna wrestled the bear and snatched the gem away. The bear was so impressed by Krishna's strength, that he let Krishna marry his daughter, Jambavati.

When he returned, Surajit apologized for suspecting Krishna and impressed with his intelligence and strength gave him his daughter's hand in marriage. Thus, Satyabhama became Krishna's wife, and brought into Krishna's household her father's vast wealth.

Satyabhama's other suitors were so upset that they murdered Surajit. Krishna tracked the killers and brought them to justice. He then requested Satyabhama to give up claims on the Syamantaka jewel and let it be shared by the entire Yadava community, as it brought nothing but bad luck to its owners.

- This story comes from Bhagavata Purana.
- Krishna gets wives in many ways: Rukmini asks him to help

her elope, Jambavati is given by her father who is impressed by his strength, Satyabhama is given by her father to make amends, Satya is a trophy after Krishna wins a bull fight, Mitravinda chooses him, Lakshman is abducted by him, Bhadra is given to him by her brothers. Then he gives refuge to 16,100 women who were abducted by Naraka, and have nowhere to go.

- There are different kinds of wedding as per dharma-shastras: the way of Prajapati (where the groom's father approaches), the Brahma (where the bride's father approaches), the Deva (where the daughter is the fee or trophy given to the son-in-law for services rendered), the Rishi (where the father enables a hermit become a householder), the Gandharva (where lovers choose each other), the Rakshasa (where women are abducted), the Asura (where women are bought) and the Pisacha (where women are raped).

24. Horses for Satyavati

Rishi Ruchika had to repay his debt to ancestors. So, he went to King Gandhi and asked for a wife. The king offered his daughter, Satyavati, but demanded a thousand horses in exchange. White horses with one black ear.

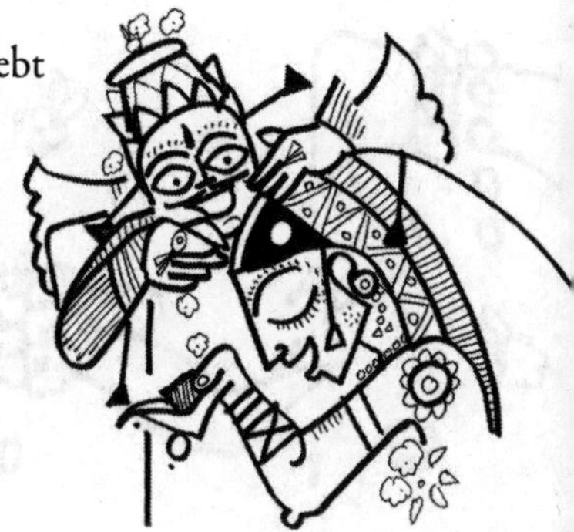

Rishi Ruchika prayed to Varuna and secured the horses and gave them to the king who let him marry his daughter, whose grandson would be the famous Parashuram.

- This story comes from the Mahabharata.
- It is difficult to classify this wedding. Ideally, the king should help a hermit become a householder. But here the daughter is being sold. This makes it Asura-vivah. So, the neat eight-fold classification of marriages found in dharma-shastra is more theory than actual.

25. Agastya Finds a Source of Income

Rishi Agastya had to repay his debt to ancestors and so went to the king of Vidarbha and asked for a wife. He was given Lopamudra. Lopamudra agreed to be a wife, if he behaved like a husband and gave her a house that was worthy of her, and bathed and dressed as a husband should, and secured an income by which they could feed their children.

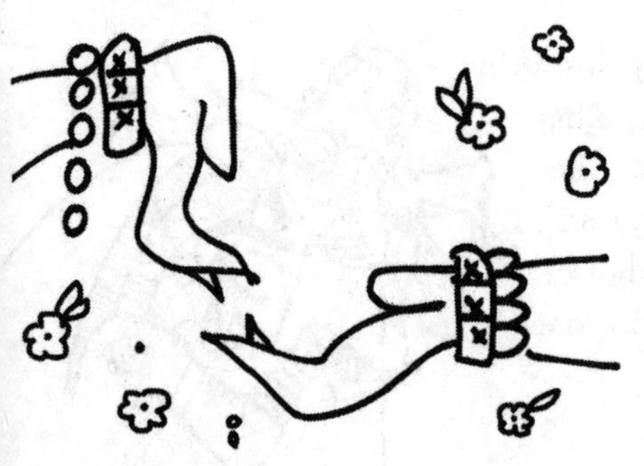

So, Agastya had to go around the world looking for income. He went to the asura-king Atapi seeking gold. 'First, you must have a meal,' said the rich king. Agastya knew what the king was up to.

Atapi would tell his brother

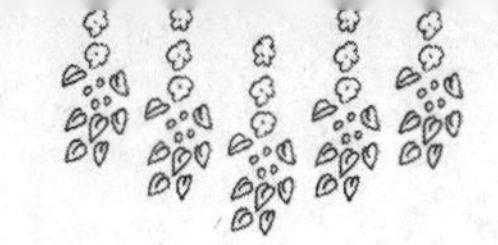

Vatapi to turn into a goat, who would be slaughtered and whose meat would be cooked and served to the guest. After the guest had eaten the meat, Atapi would call out to Vatapi and Vatapi would reform as a goat in the stomach of his guest and tear his way out, killing the guest in the process.

Unfortunately for Atapi, Agastya had wonderful digestive powers. He digested Vatapi before Atapi could call him out. Atapi had no choice but to give the promised gold to Agastya. Later, Agastya drank waters of a lake to reveal to the devas that asuras could be killed. In gratitude, the devas gave him gold too. With this gold, Agastya could build a house for Lopamudra, and approach her dressed as a worthy groom, and get an income for their children.

- This story has its roots in Rig Veda but is elaborated in later Puranic tales and even in Tamil literature.
- Agastya marries to repay debt to ancestors but ends up a householder, helping solve worldly problems, to earn a living.

26. Sita Marries Ram

King Janaka had the bow of Shiva that no one could lift, except his daughter Sita. He declared that whosoever could lift this bow and string it would marry her. Many came but all failed, including Ravana, king of Lanka, who almost got crushed under the weight of the bow.

Ram, son of Dashrath, of the solar dynasty, came with his teacher Vishwamitra and asked to see the bow. He was able to lift it and he bent the bow to string it but such was his strength that the bow broke in two.

As he had proved his strength, Ram was given Sita as his wife.

- This story comes from the Ramayana.
- In Valmiki Ramayana, there is no great ceremony where all kings gather to string the bow; that detail is added later to make the event more theatrical.
- A woman choosing a husband (swayamvar) was confused with a woman becoming a trophy of a martial tournament. Control of choosing husband shifted from the girl to her father. This reminds us of the verses in Manusmriti that say a woman must always be dependent on father, brother, husband or son.

27. Ganga Marries Shantanu

When King Mahabhisha was invited to Indra's paradise Swarga, he was so smitten by Ganga's beauty that he ignored Indra. This upset Indra. He told Mahabhisha that he would be reborn on earth and Ganga would break his heart.

Ganga, the river-goddess, waited for Shantanu's birth on earth. One day, she saw a man just like him on her riverbank. She went and sat on his right lap and asked him to marry her. The man refused saying, 'I have given up the householder's way and renounced my kingdom. I am a hermit now. So, I cannot marry you. Also, you sat on my right thigh, not my left, and so I can only look upon you as daughter or daughter-in-law. You may marry my son, Shantanu. That is my advice.'

Shantanu saw Ganga and was smitten by her beauty. Ganga agreed to be his wife but on condition that he never question her actions. Shantanu agreed, and they became husband and wife.

What Shantanu did not expect was his wife would kill their newborn babies. When he stopped her from killing the eighth child, she left him and returned to the gods. 'The son you saved will never be husband, and so cannot be king,' she said before leaving. 'That is a fate worse than death.'

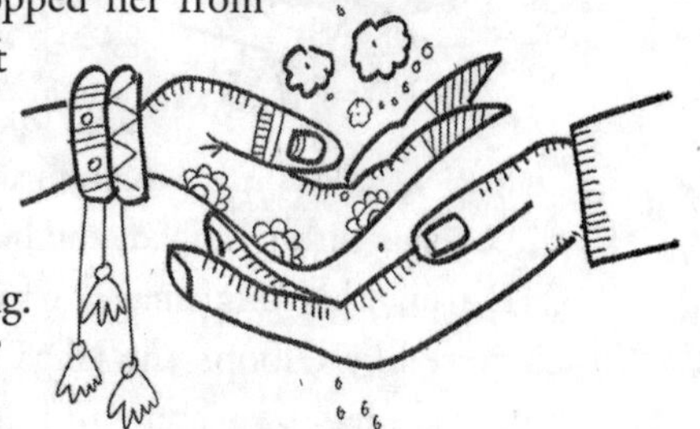

- This story comes from the Mahabharata.
- Both the Ramayana and the Mahabharata warn men, especially kings, from promising anything to women.

Ganga demands freedom and uses that power to kill her own children. In the Ramayana, Kaikeyi uses the boons her husband gives her to prevent the coronation of the eldest prince, Ram.

28. Uloopi Marries Arjuna

Arjuna shared his wife Draupadi with his five brothers and they had agreed that when she was with one brother, the other brothers would look upon her as their sister-in-law.

Once, searching for his bow, Arjuna entered Draupadi's chambers when she was with his eldest brother, Yudhishtira. For this crime, Arjuna had to go on a pilgrimage for 12 long years, which meant his four brothers would have three turns with Draupadi and he would have none.

During this pilgrimage, while bathing in a river, he was abducted by Uloopi, the Naga princess. She took him to her palace under the waters and asked him to marry her. They spent a passionate night together and from the union was born Iravan.

- This story comes from the Mahabharata.
- This may be called Gandharva-vivah as it is based on mutual consent and does not involve family.

29. Chitrangada Marries Arjuna

During his pilgrimage, Arjuna went to Manipur famous for its warrior princess Chitrangada.

Chitrangada, looked like a man, and behaved like a man. She fell in love with Arjuna, when he arrived in her kingdom. Fearing he would not find her feminine enough she prayed to Shiva to strip her of her manly traits. Thus, adequately feminized, she approached Arjuna, but unfortunately, he had no interest in her. He was more interested in wooing the masculine princess, who could hunt wild boars in the forest, that he had heard so much about in his travels. On hearing this, Chitrangada begged Shiva to restore her to her original form. Arjuna fell in love with this princess with a bow instantly.

But Chitrangada's father, Chitravahana, had a condition. The son born of their union would belong not to Arjuna but to Chitravahana, who had no son. Arjuna agreed and so the son born of this union, Babruvahana, was adopted by his maternal grandfather.

- This story comes from the Mahabharata.
- In many communities of ancient India, the child belonged to the mother not the father. She controlled the land.

30. Subhadra Marries Arjuna

Balarama had taught wrestling to Duryodhana and wanted him to marry his sister, Subhadra. But Subhadra wanted to marry Arjuna and so when Arjuna visited Dwarka, she ran away with him. On Krishna's advice, she held the reins of the chariot to let her brothers know that she was eloping with Arjuna; he was not abducting her.

But Arjuna had a problem. He shared his first wife, Draupadi, with his four brothers. She had agreed to be the common wife provided the brothers did not bring any of their other wives into the household. How could Arjuna now get Subhadra to stay with him in Indraprastha?

Krishna's sister had a plan. Disguised as a milkmaid, she went to Draupadi's palace and told her tragic tale, how she had no home as she had eloped from her father's house with her lover, and her lover's first wife would not let her enter his house. Feeling sorry for her, Draupadi offered Subhadra shelter in her palace, not knowing she was the first wife being referred to. Thus, was Draupadi tricked to accept Arjuna's wife in her household.

- This story comes from the Mahabharata and Bhagavata Purana.

- This is a cousin marriage. Arjuna's mother and Subhadra's father are siblings.
- Many communities in India forbid marriages between sa-pinda (common grandfathers, great grandfathers) and between sa-gotra (same clan).
- While North Indians forbid marriage between cousins, it is common in South India, especially in land-owning families, to ensure the land remains in the extended family.

31. Arjuna Marries Ali

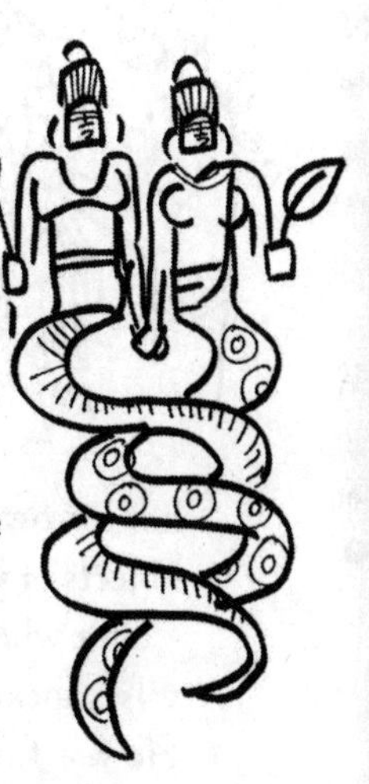

The Tamil queen Ali would not marry. She ruled her country wisely and had no need of a man. Arjuna fell in love with her and wanted to marry. All his attempts at wooing her failed. So, he asked for Krishna's help.

Krishna turned Arjuna into a snake so that he could slip into the queen's royal bedchamber and make love to her while she slept. Arjuna's passionate lovemaking made Ali so happy that she agreed to be Arjuna's wife.

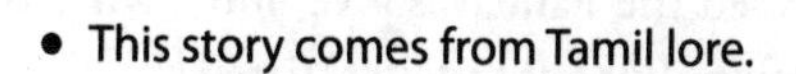

- This story comes from Tamil lore.
- This can be classified as Pisacha-vivah, marriage by rape, following the way of ghosts and goblins. Though forbidden in dharma-shastra this story suggests 'all is fair in love and war' and so may not appeal to modern sentiment.

- After the seduction, Ali falls in love with Arjuna, and loses her masculine nature.

32. The Passion of Poramannan

Draupadi, wife of the five Pandava brothers, who had been publicly humiliated by Duryodhana, the Kaurava, vowed not to tie her hair until she could use Duryodhana's thigh bone as her comb. She was told that the defeat of Duryodhana would be possible only if her husbands obtained a sacred whip, sword, drum, casket and lamp belonging to a warlord called Gurulingam.

To get these sacred artifacts, Arjuna, Draupadi's favourite husband, approached Gurulingam's son Pormannan disguised as a beautiful girl called Vijayampal and enticed him with her charms. Pormannan agreed to kill his own father Gurulingam and give Vijayampal the sacred objects of worship if she became his wife.

But when the deed was done and the gifts given, Poramannan was shocked to find that his beloved Vijayampal was a man. He was furious and demanded the Pandavas give him a wife, as Arjuna had aroused his passions but left him unsatiated.

The Pandavas gave him their younger sister, Shankuvati. Poramannan became the guardian of his sister-in-law Draupadi and helped her forces defeat Duryodhana.

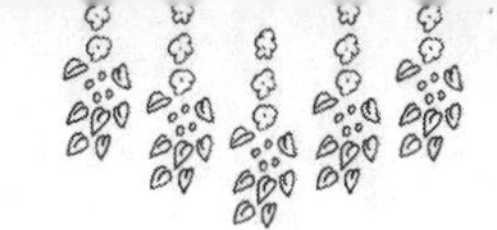

- This story comes from the Tamil Mahabharata.
- Here, we find that trickery and the promise of marriage is used by heroes to defeat the villain.
- Poramannan realizes that he is not desirable; he is simply useful. Luckily, for him, the Pandavas give him a wife in the end.

33. Pradyumna Marries Mayavati

Krishna and Rukmini had a son called Pradyumna. As soon as he was born, he was kidnapped by the asura-king Shambara and thrown into a river.

A fish swallowed him, which was later caught and taken to the kitchen of Shambara's palace. Shambara's wife, Mayavati, cut open the fish and found inside it a beautiful baby boy. She raised him secretly in the kitchen.

When the boy grew up, he was so handsome that Mayavati fell in love with him and sought to marry him. Pradyumna hesitated. Mayavati then told him the story of his birth. She also told him that she was actually Rati, the goddess of love, whose husband, Kama, had been burnt to ashes by Shiva's third eye. She revealed that he was Kama reborn and so they were already married.

Mayavati revealed to Pradyumna his secret powers. Thus armed, Pradyumna challenged Shambara to a duel, killed him, claimed his queen Mayavati as his wife, and returned to Dwarka to meet his parents where everyone recognized him as he looked just like Krishna.

- This story comes from the Harivamsa and Bhagavata Purana.
- In Jain versions of this tale, Pradyumna rejects Mayavati's offer and considers her a demon.
- In the Hindu version, the older woman seducing a younger man, and the incestuous undertones, are overlooked on the grounds that Mayavati and Pradyumna are Rati and Kama reborn.

34. Usha Marries Aniruddha

The asura-princess, Usha, asked her friend, the sorceress and artist Chitralekha, to find her the most handsome man on earth. Chitralekha travelled around the world and found Aniruddha, grandson of Krishna, who lived in Dwaravati. Dwaravati, in the west, was far from her house in the east, in Shonitapura. Smitten by his beauty, Usha decided to abduct Aniruddha. Aniruddha was more than pleased to be selected by Usha. Unfortunately, Usha's father Bana hated Aniruddha's grandfather Krishna and opposed the match. He threw Aniruddha in prison.

Usha sent word to Krishna of her plight and Krishna came flying on his eagle named Garuda along with his brother, Balarama, and his sons, Pradyumna and Samba, and they battled Bana who was joined by Shiva and Kali. Is a father's hatred more important than a daughter's love, asked Krishna? Kali said no. And so, the war stopped, and the couple was united, and Aniruddha became Bana's son-in-law and Usha became Krishna's daughter-in-law.

- The idea of a man being abducted by a woman is not common but is found in Bhagavata literature.
- Puranas repeatedly speak of women abandoning their husbands for a handsome youth. Thus, Shiva is irresistible. So is Krishna, his son Pradyumna, and his grandson Aniruddha.
- The idea of women's desire is highlighted in Sanskrit literature. Later, it is seen as dangerous and in need of control. Eventually, women are made to feel ashamed of their desire. It is assumed men have desires, and women have to submit to it, rather than being equal participants.

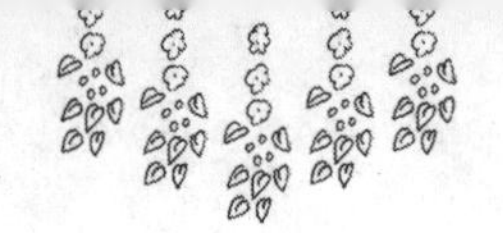

35. Sasirekha's Marriage

When the Pandavas lost their kingdom in a game of dice and were forced into forest exile, all the Pandava children took shelter in Dwarka, Subhadra's son Abhimanyu being one amongst them. At his uncle's house, Abhimanyu met his cousin, Sasirekha, Balarama's daughter and they fell in love.

Unfortunately, Balarama opposed the match. Since Duryodhana could not marry his sister, he argued that to maintain cordial relations between the Kauravas and the Yadavas, his daughter should be given in marriage to Duryodhana's son, Laxman.

Not wanting to oppose his elder brother openly, Krishna enlisted the help of Bhima's son Ghatotkacha to unite Abhimanyu and Sasirekha. During the wedding, Ghatotkacha used his magical powers and took the form of Sasirekha. While Laxman got married to the false Sasirekha in the public arena, the real Sasirekha married Abhimanyu in the private quarters, to the sound of the same wedding chants. By the time the trick was discovered, it was too late.

- This story is part of Bhagavata Purana and oral traditions.
- This is a cousin wedding. Abhimanyu's mother Subhadra and Sasirekha's father Balarama are siblings.
- These stories probably originated in South India where cousin marriage is common.

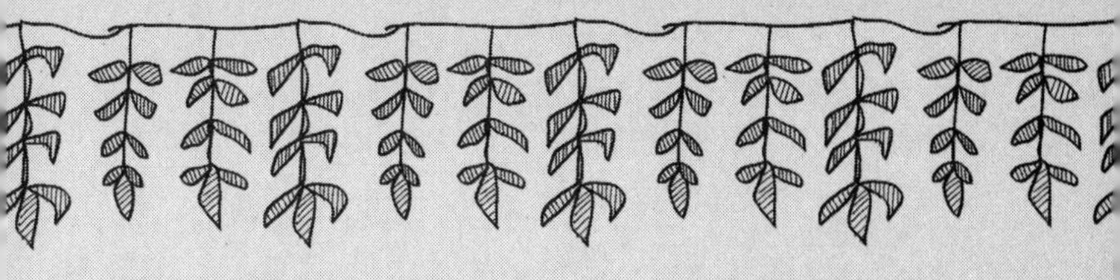

IV

Fidelity

Stories from the Ramayana and the Mahabharata reveal the anxiety of men over women's fidelity. This is at odds with the Rig Veda that introduces us to Indrani, who is not so true to her husband, and to Urvashi, who leaves her husband in search of paradise. A chaste wife who dies before her husband is worshipped as a goddess. She dies 'sadhava' and finds a place in the afterlife in Gauri-loka, reserved for fertile matriarchs.

36. Oghavati

While stepping out of the house, Oghavati's husband, Sudarshan, told her, 'Should a guest arrive in my absence, take care of all his needs.' While he was away, a guest did arrive, but his needs were a bit excessive. He wanted to have sex with her, to which Oghavati agreed.

While the two were thus engaged, Sudarshan returned home. 'Wife, where are you?' he asked. Oghavati was too shy to reply. So, the guest shouted from inside that she was busy with her guest on her husband's bed attending to the guest's needs. Sudarshan politely waited outside until the guest was ready to leave. The guest blessed the couple for their generous hospitality, and revealed he was Dharma, god of civilized conduct.

- This story comes from the Mahabharata and takes hospitality to another level.
- Treating strangers and guests is the sign of a good

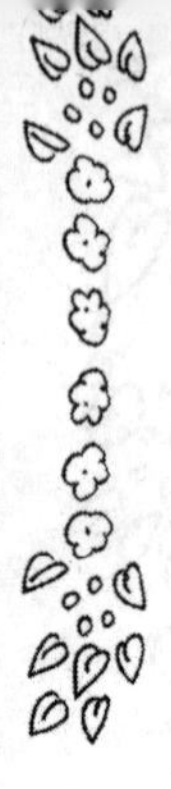

household not just in Vedic culture but also ancient Greek and Abrahamic culture.

- Manu says that the purpose of the household is to feed everyone: self, family, strangers, guests, gods and ancestors. But what does 'food' mean?
- In a story found in the Mahabharata, the sage Raibhya punishes Yavakri for having sex with his daughter-in-law, Paravasu's wife. The woman is not condemned; only the man.
- The Mahabharata tells the story of how Brihaspati tries to have sex with his sister-in-law. The act is not condemned. The sister-in-law, Mamata, stops him only because she is already pregnant. Brihaspati is furious and condemns the child in her womb to be born blind.

37. Bhartrihari's Wife

King Bhartrihari of Ujjain was given a jewel that he gave to his wife. The next day, he found the jewel on a heap of elephant dung being carried by a scavenger woman.

'Who gave it to you?' he asked the lady.

'The elephant stable keeper gave it to me. He is my lover,' said the lady.

Bhartrihari confronted the elephant stable keeper and he revealed with great hesitation that it was the queen herself who gave the jewel to him. 'Every night she gives you a drink that makes you sleep and while you are asleep, she comes into the elephant stable asking me to satisfy her.'

Bhartrihari was heartbroken on hearing this. He realized love is an illusion. He renounced his kingdom and let his brother Vikramaditya rule the kingdom instead.

- Bhartrihari's story is popular in Sanskrit literature as well as regional literature of the Deccan.
- These stories are from the Nath-jogi traditions that see householder's life as full of sensuality, lack of morals and general lasciviousness. Women are unfaithful. Husbands are unfaithful.
- The wife's infidelity turns the king into an ascetic. He does not condemn the wife. This is very unlike Gautama's reaction in the Ramayana when he finds his wife, Ahalya, in bed with Indra. He curses her to turn into stone and curses Indra that his body will be covered with open sores.
- In Yoga Vasishtha, king Shikhidhvaja feels women cannot teach yoga and that yoga cannot be taught in a palace. So, he goes into the forest looking for a teacher. His wife, Chudala, expert in yoga and tantra, takes the form of a man and becomes his teacher in the forest. Then this man turns into a woman and asks Shikhidhvaja to have sex with her and satisfy her longings. Shikhidhavja complies, giving pleasure to the woman without taking pleasure himself. Then he finds her with another man, and does not mind it. Later he rejects Indra's paradise declaring paradise is where the mind is wise. Chudala then reveals herself and

praises him for learning yoga and controlling his mind. He is adequately detached, not entitled, and realizes paradise can be found anywhere, forest or palace.

38. Renuka

When Jamadagni would shoot an arrow, his wife, Renuka, would run fast and catch it before it hit the ground. But one day, she returned home late. When asked why, she said that the sun was burning the ground making it hard to walk. This made Jamadagni so angry he threatened to shoot the sun down. The sun told the sage a simpler solution would be to give his wife, who he loved so much, an umbrella and a pair of slippers to protect her from the heat.

Renuka was devoted to Jamadagni and thought of no one but him. She was so chaste that she gained the power to collect water from unbaked pots. But then one day she saw a handsome king bathing in a river, and for a moment she entertained adulterous thoughts. Her husband, Jamadagni, divined this and ordered his sons to behead her.

Four of his five sons, refused. The fifth one agreed. He raised his axe and beheaded Renuka and so became known as Parashuram, the Ram who wields an axe. His four elder brothers, who refused to kill their mother, became eunuchs.

Parashuram begged his father to bring his mother back to life. Brought back to life, she became known as the goddess Yellamma.

- This story is found in the Mahabharata, in the Puranas and in many regional folklore.

- Parashuram is never visualized as a married man. He is never worshipped independently. His shrine is a subsidiary shrine in Renuka's temple complex.

- Medieval Sanskrit literature is full of stories of clever adulteresses. They are found in collections such as Kathasaritsagar (ocean of stories). There are tales of how women having affairs use tricks and manage to escape punishment. Tricks are also used by men who want their wives to stop having affairs. For example, a woman tells her lover to dress as a madman and asks her to touch her in public. She then announces that no man other than her husband and the madman have ever touched her. The yaksha-of-truth agrees, and her husband is convinced she is not the adulteress everyone claims she is. When a barber finds out that the king is sleeping with his wife, he tells the king that his wife is a witch who sucks out entrails from a man's anus, eats undigested food and shoves the entrails back in the body each night. He then tells his wife that the king's anus has teeth. The next time the king meets the barber's wife he notices her trying to check out his anus and is convinced she is indeed a witch.

- A merchant goes on a long voyage and is sure that in his absence his wife will have affairs with other men. So, he leaves behind a parrot who, every night, for the entire night, tells his wife stories of love and betrayal and fidelity. Spellbound by the stories the wife never leaves the house.

Thus, she remains chaste. The collection of these stories is called *Suka Saptati*, seventy tales of the parrot.

39. The Jambul Fruit

Draupadi, common wife of the five Pandavas, plucked a Jambul without realizing that it was a special fruit that a sage had sworn to break his fast of twelve years with.

'Fix it back,' the sage demanded. 'It can be done if you tell a truth you have shared with no one.'

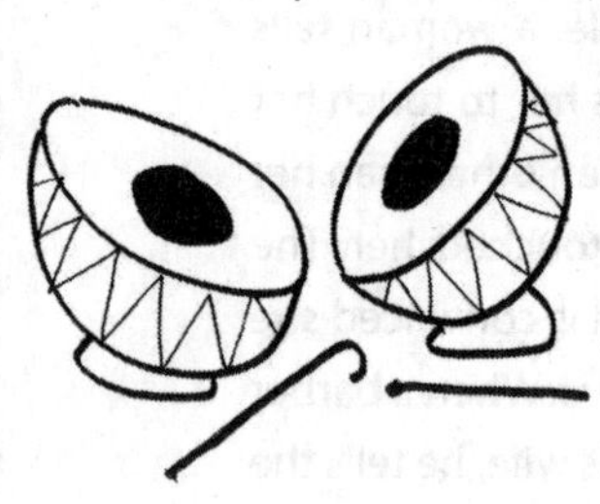

With great trepidation, Draupadi looked into the eyes of her husbands and said, 'I love five of you. But I love a sixth too. I love Karna, the charioteer who serves Duryodhana. I regret not marrying him on account of his origins.' Having revealed the truth of her heart, Draupadi had been cleansed. She was now able to refix the fruit to the tree and the Rishi was able to break his fast.

The revelation came as a shock to the Pandavas. They were not sure whether to be angry with Draupadi or ashamed of themselves. Had they failed her individually and collectively?

Later Draupadi was cast in Naraka briefly as she favoured Arjuna over her other husbands.

- This is a folklore from Maharashtra. It explains why the Indian blackberry stains the mouth purple—as we all have secrets, like Draupadi.

- It reminds us that desire cannot be contained by marriage. Even when a woman has many husbands, she may desire more. Likewise, a man with many wives, is never satisfied. Satisfaction is not a function of the wife or wives. It is about how much control we have on our minds.
- In Bengali folklore, when Draupadi wails at her misfortune, how despite having five husbands no one came to her rescue when she was abused by Kauravas, then Jayadhrata and then Kichaka, Krishna tells her that he wanted her to marry Karna. But Draupadi had rejected Karna because he did not know who his biological parents were, while she chose Arjuna even though he was disguised as a priest. Thus, we are drawn by things that are not good for us and repulsed by things that are good for us. Similar comments are made by Ravana before he dies.

40. Chyavana and Sukanya

Sukanya saw a pair of fireflies inside a termite hill. She tried to catch them with a stick and ended up piercing the eyes of a hermit who was deep in meditation in that termite hill, which had formed around him. For this crime, her father told her to become the caretaker of the sage, whose name was Chyavana.

Thus, a young and beautiful princess became wife of an old, withered ascetic.

The handsome Ashwin twins appeared before Sukanya and sought her hand in marriage. She refused. She wanted to be true to her husband. Impressed, the twin gods took Chyavana for a bath in the river. All three lowered their heads in water, and when they emerged, all three looked the same. 'Choose your husband,' they told Sukanya.

Sukanya realized this was a test. She knew the gods do not blink and so was able to identify Chyavana easily. She chose the mortal over the immortals and was blessed by the gods.

- This is one of the earliest stories of fidelity in Vedic literature.
- Sukanya means the good girl. She obeys her parents. She cares for her husband even though he is old and blind and ugly. She resists temptations.
- Sukanya's story is different from Lopamudra, the demanding wife, and Urvashi, the fickle wife.

41. Vrinda

The asura-king Jalandhara was married to Vrinda, who was so faithful to him in action and thought that her fidelity gave her powers to protect her husband from harm. Protected by his wife's fidelity, Jalandhara went about troubling everyone in the three worlds. The devas complained to Vishnu.

So, Vishnu took the form of Jalandhara and went to Vrinda's

house and she treated him as a wife treats a husband, not realizing this was an imposter. As a result, she was no longer chaste. Her powers waned and the devas were able to kill Jalandhara.

Vrinda was angry as she had been tricked. In grief, she turned into the tulsi plant. Vishnu, who had acted out of necessity, declared that Vrinda will never be seen as a widow. She would be worshipped in the courtyard of every household by married women whose husbands are still alive (sadhava, sumangali).

- This story is found in the Puranas.
- The idea of wife protecting the health of the husband encouraged the practice of preventing widow remarriage and encouraging 'sati' where the widow burnt herself on the husband's funeral pyre.
- In Hindu households, the tulsi is kept in the courtyard and worshipped as the chaste wife by the matriarch of the household. Perhaps in ancient times, married women who died before their husbands (sadhava, sumangali) were buried in courtyard and the spot was marked by a tulsi plant. Even today holy men are buried so, in seated position. Such women go to the abode of chaste wives, Gauri-loka, and protect the household.
- There are stories in folk Ramayana of how Ravana's wives are infatuated by vanaras and so are unable to protect Ravana from Ram's arrows.

- Fasting for husband's health is an integral ritual followed by Hindu housewives. The 'Chhat' festival in Bihar is where the matriarch prays for the entire household's welfare.

42. Kannagi and Kovalan

Kannagi suffered silently while her husband Kovalan spent all his time with a courtesan. When all his money was gone, the courtesan threw Kovalan out of her house. Penniless, Kovalan turned to family and friends for help. They all rejected the philanderer. Only Kannagi stood by him. Together they set out to the city of Madurai to start afresh.

To help Kovalan raise capital for his business, Kannagi gave him one of her gold anklets. When Kovalan offered this anklet for sale in the market, the goldsmiths accused him of stealing the queen's jewellery. They took him to the king who ordered his immediate execution.

When Kannagi learnt how her husband had been put to death, she strode into the royal palace, presented her other anklet, proved her husband's innocence and demanded justice. 'Give me back my husband,' she cried.

When there was no response, she plucked off one of her breasts and hurled it into the city square. Instantly the whole city of Madurai was engulfed in flames. All its residents—who had stood by silently while Kannagi's innocent husband was being put to death—were burnt alive. Tales of how Kannagi destroyed

the city of Madurai spread across the countryside. Residents of neighbouring villages enshrined her images in temples and began worshipping her as a goddess named Pattani, the chaste wife.

- This is one of the earliest stories from Tamil literature that draws attention to the powers of a chaste wife, making her more powerful than the courtesan and the nun. The epic story is called Shilapaddikaram, or the golden anklets.
- Kannagi is called the chaste wife and worshipped as Pattani.
- In Puranic literature, we find women like Shilavati who are so true to their husbands that they can stop even the sun from rising. They are true to their husbands despite the fact that husbands are diseased, uncaring, violent and even unfaithful. A wife's fidelity is thus linked to life and fortune of the husband. She may call him husband-god (pati-parmeshwara) but she is the household goddess of fortune (griha-lakshmi).

43. Anasuya and the Birth of Dattatreya

Anasuya was a chaste wife, devoted to her husband Atri. To test her chastity, Brahma, Vishnu and Shiva came before her in the form of three handsome ascetics and declared that they had been fasting for twelve years and to break their fast they need a chaste woman to breast feed them.

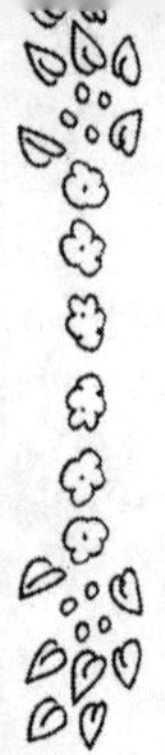

Anasuya agreed but clarified that she had no children and so her breasts had no milk. As soon as the three men came forward to suckle her breasts, they turned into three children and milk poured out of Anasuya's breasts.

The three gods acknowledged the chastity of Anasuya and apologized for their trickery. They blessed her with a son, Dattatreya, teacher of Nath-jogis, who contained the power of Brahma, Vishnu and Shiva.

- This story comes from the Nath-jogi tradition. Dattatreya is Adi-guru, teacher of teachers.
- In folk narratives, Saraswati, Lakshmi and Durga are jealous of Anasuya's chastity and so send their husbands Brahma, Vishnu and Shiva to destroy her power. But they fail. Thus, the Nath-jogis claim they have more power than mainstream Hindu gods.
- In Indian folklore, vira is a man with many wives but a greater hero (maha-vira) is one who has no need for wives. Similarly, Shiva is maha-deva and greater than regular gods (devas) as he is an ascetic and seeks neither food nor wife.

44. Arundhati

Each of the seven primal sages, who constitute the Sapta Rishi mandal, had a wife. One day, the god of fire, Agni, saw them and fell in love with them and desired them. Fearing her husband would disrespect the chaste women, Agni's wife Svaha took the form of the sage-wives and satisfied Agni's lust. She could take the form of six of the seven wives, not that of Arundhati, wife of Vasishtha.

From this union were born six children, who merged to become one. This child with six heads started to cry and the breasts of six of the seven sage-wives started to ooze milk. The Rishis accused these six of infidelity. The women insisted they were chaste. Angry with their husbands they moved away and confronted the wretched child who revealed the secret of his birth.

The child, Skanda, who became warlord of the gods, told the six women, they would become the Kritika constellation of six stars in the sky and the Matrika goddesses on earth. Those who did not respect them would lose their children to miscarriage and fevers.

- This is one of the earliest stories of infidelity from Vedic lore. It explains why the Big Dipper is in the centre of the sky and the Pleiades is at the horizon.
- Some Vedic communities did not mind polyandry or a woman's many lovers and husbands. But others were more rigid and valued the faithful wife. Thus, we see diversity even in Vedic culture. Just as some Vedic sages ate meat, perhaps even beef, while others shunned all kinds of meat.
- In the Mahabharata, it is said the Sapta Rishis had one wife, Jatila.

45. Ashtavakra's Fidelity

Sage Vadanya refused to let Ashtavakra marry his daughter Suprabha until he had paid a visit to the abode of damsels, stri-rajya, and spoken to its ruler, the beautiful Uttara. Vadanya wanted to be sure that his future son-in-law was marrying his daughter for reasons other than physical pleasures.

When Ashtavakra reached the abode of damsels, located to the north of the Himalayas, Uttara welcomed him enthusiastically. She spoke at length on subjects ranging from love to erotica. When Ashtavakra prepared to leave, she begged him to stay back and marry her. She offered

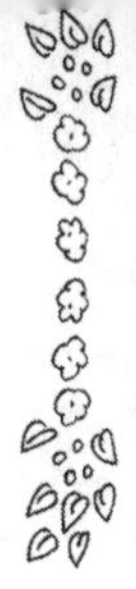

him physical pleasures that were beyond human imagination. Ashtavakra refused as his heart belonged to Suprabha.

Instead of getting angry, Uttara smiled. She revealed that she had been asked by Vadanya to test his resolve. She blessed Ashtavakra and wished him a happy married life.

- This story comes from the Mahabharata and reveals how chaste wives, even chaste husbands, are admired.
- In Hindu mythology, Ram is the only god venerated for being faithful to one wife, ekam-patni-vrata. He has one wife (ekapatni), uses one arrow to hit his target (ekabani) and always is true to his word (ekabani).
- The story of damsels seducing ascetics is a recurring theme in Puranas. Vishwamitra is seduced by Menaka but resists the charm of Rambha. Here the point is not to be faithful to a wife. Here the point is sensory control. The ascetic is called tapasvi (he who churns fire) and the damsel is called apsara (she who is born of water). The damsel is thus water to the ascetic's fire. She can douse him or he can evaporate her.
- The tension between men and women gives rise to many stories which later were translated into Arabic and came to be known as Tuti-nama, or tales of the parrot. In India, they are called tota-mynah (parrot-mynah) stories with the parrot arguing for the man and the mynah arguing for the woman.

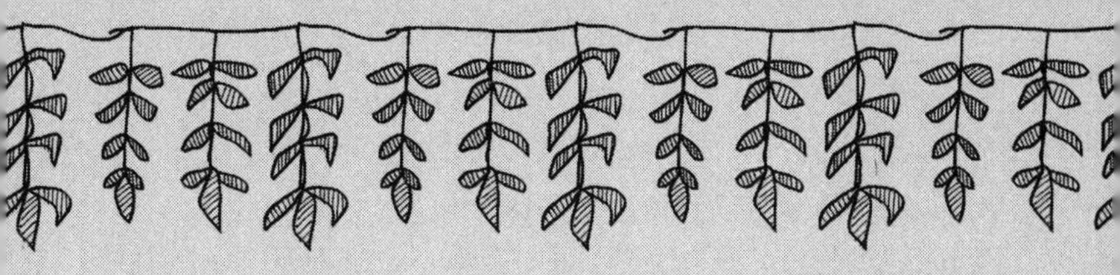

V

Multiplicity

In the Vedic wedding hymn, the wife is first given to Soma, then to a gandharva, then to Agni, and finally bound firmly to the mortal groom. Does it capture an ancient memory of polyandry? In temples, only gods are polygamous: for uniting diverse realms, binding diverse communities and satisfying diverse needs.

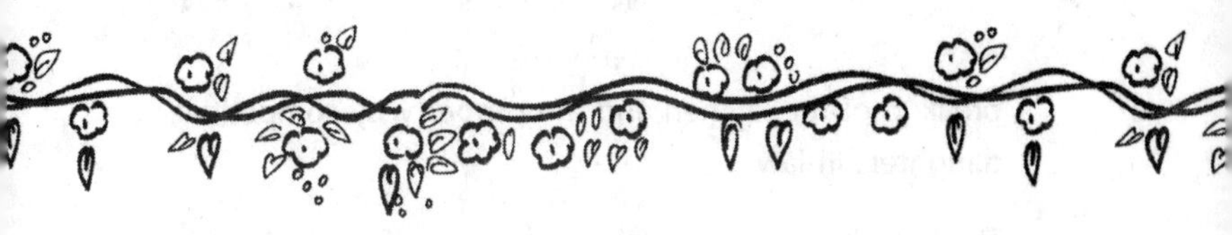

46. Pracheta Brothers Find a Wife

The ten Pracheta brothers meditated for many years under the sea. When they emerged, they saw plants had covered the whole world. Furious, they decided to burn all the trees.

The plants created the perfect woman, Marisha, and she married the ten Pracheta brothers. And from that union of one woman with many men was born Daksha who married many women, who gave him daughters, who he gave to the gods, who in turn ensured the well-being of the world.

- This story is found in the Puranas. It is one of the many examples of polyandry (one woman marrying many men) found in scriptures.
- Draupadi's five husbands is the most popular case of polyandry. To convince her to marry the brothers, she is told about Jatila who married the Sapta Rishis, and about Bhaumasvi who married many kings.
- In many communities, a wife was shared to prevent

breakup of the kitchen and the property by competitive daughters-in-law.

- The Mahabharata argues that sharing a wife is dangerous: Tilotamma was sent by Indra to drive a wedge between the brothers Sunda and Upasunda. Both brothers wanted her and ended up killing each other.

47. The Secret Life of Draupadi

The Pandava Bhima complained to Krishna that he could not satisfy his wife sexually and felt inadequate as a result. Krishna revealed to Bhima that their wife was the primal mother goddess Adya-Maya-Shakti.

One night, the Pandavas discovered that Draupadi was not in her bed. They searched the forest and discovered her running, wild and naked in the forest, eating goats, buffaloes and other

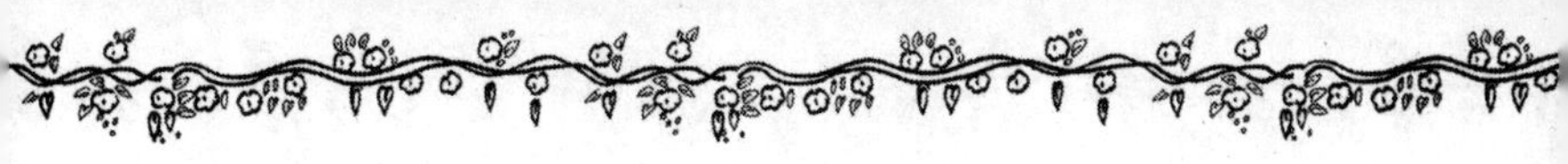

wild animals. When she realized that her husbands were spying on her, she ran towards them, intending to catch and eat them too.

The Pandavas ran for cover and sought refuge in their palace. They shut the door and refused to let Draupadi in until she promised not to harm them. She agreed and Bhima opened the door.

Draupadi gripped his hand so hard that her five fingernails pierced his skin and five drops of blood fell on the ground. These turned into children and hearing them cry, Draupadi's fury abated and she became maternal and loving once again.

- This story comes from the Tamil Mahabharata.
- Similar tales are found in the Bhil Mahabharata where Draupadi is described as a goddess served by Indra and Brahma who sweep the floor, massage her feet, and bow to her.
- The Bhil Mahabharata acknowledges that women have greater sexual appetites and so are free to go to other men if their husband cannot satisfy them. And so, Indra's wife, unsatisfied with her husband, makes love to Abhimanyu. And in one tale, Arjuna watches while Vasuki, the snake-god makes love to Draupadi. These stories are told matter-of-factly with no outrage or shame.
- There is a constant need to explain Draupadi's polyandry. One reason is that in her previous life she was Nalayani whose husband took many forms of different kinds of men to satisfy her, but she remained dissatisfied and would

not let him renounce the world. He got so upset that he cursed her to be reborn as a woman with five dedicated husbands. In another story, she asks Shiva for a husband with five great qualities. Shiva gives her five husbands each with one great quality.

48. Dhola Fetches Maru

Dhola was the son of Raja Nala and his queen, Damayanti. He was given in marriage to Maru, when he was a child. As was custom, Maru stayed with her parents until she would mature enough to go to her husband's house.

Years passed. Dhola grew up to be a young man. One day, he killed a parrot that belonged to Rewa, a sorceress, who was in love with him, but he had consistently ignored her. When he was fishing at the lake, he never saw her fetch water, even though she came seven times. Rewa demanded that Dhola stay in her palace and give her company, as she had lost her only companion, the parrot. Dhola had no choice but to agree, and he eventually agreed to be Rewa's husband and stay in her palace. He forgot all about his parents and his marriage to Maru, until one day, he heard bards singing of her plight, on the street outside.

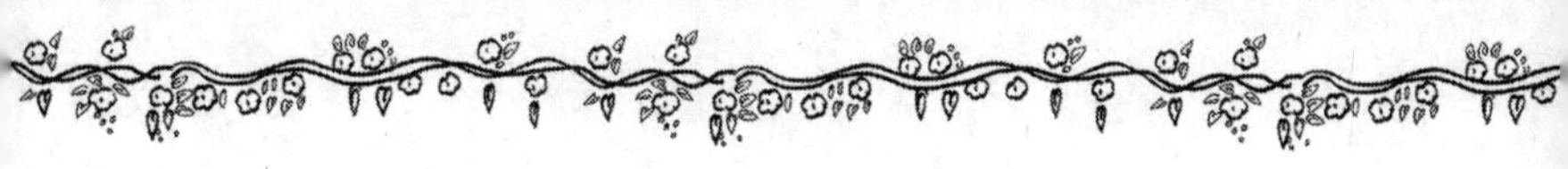

With great difficulty, Dhola managed to escape from Rewa's palace, and he travelled on a flying camel across the desert to fetch his bride. Rewa tried every trick to stop him and make him turn around. But Dhola was determined.

But at one point, during the return journey, Maru was bitten by a serpent and died. Dhola decided he would burn himself on her funeral pyre, but a jogi and a jogini, passing by revived her with their music and told them they were destined to be united.

Eventually, Dhola returned home with Maru but he also accepted the jealous Rewa as his wife and all three lived happily.

- Many versions of this ballad are found in Rajasthan and Chhattisgarh.
- Camels became popular in Rajasthan around tenth century after Muslim warlords began raiding and conquering north-western parts of India.
- It refers to the practice of child marriage and the ritual of 'gauna' or the second marriage when the girl became mature and the husband came to fetch her.
- There are many ballads of heroes who have two wives: the one he loves and the other he is obliged to marry, the one who makes him happy and the other who stresses him out.
- In Jagannath temple, Puri, Odisha, Lakshmi shuts the door of the temple and has to be appeased to let Jagannath in. She is upset as he went on a chariot ride with his sister and brother and left her behind. Such ritual enactment of domestic quarrels are part of temple lore.

49. Lorik-Chanda

Chanda was a princess married to a prince, but the prince never could make her happy. Lorik was a cowherd and he was married to a milkmaid, but she could never make him happy. One day, Chanda and Lorik met and instantly fell in love.

They spent days pining for each other and figuring out how to meet. When they met, they experienced happiness like never before.

But it was not easy as both were married. Chanda's husband tried to kill Lorik and Lorik's wife tried to get him back by saying all his cows had been stolen by neighbours.

Some say, Lorik eventually abandoned both women and became a wandering ascetic. Others say, Chanda's husband let Chanda go and live with Lorik and his wife, and the three managed to find a way to be happy together. Nobody knows for sure.

- Lorik-Chanda ballad is narrated in Chhattisgarh. There are many versions of the tale.
- It is an unusual acknowledgement of how desires are not contained by marriage.
- The story draws attention to class difference, with Chanda being a princess (a code for landowner) and Lorik being a lowly herdsman.
- Chanda's husband is described as being ill and impotent. These details are often used to justify her adultery. The common belief is that if the husband takes care of the wife's needs, her eyes will not wander, and if the wife takes

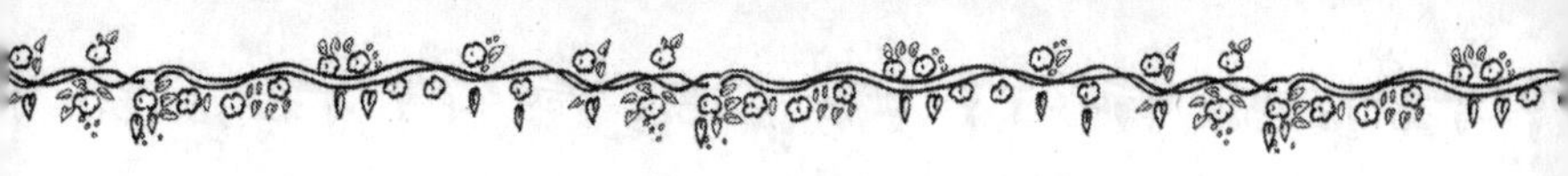

care of the husband's needs, his eyes will not wander. But life is just not that simple.

- Animal herders of Central India such as Ahirs worship Bir Kuar whose wife feels threatened by his female buffalo. The hero argues he prefers the buffalo as she nods when he speaks, while his human wife does not even listen to him.

50. Murugan's Valli

They say that Skanda also known as Murugan, the son of Shiva and Shakti, moved south because his parents got his younger brother married before him. There in the South, he killed many demons and married Devasena, the daughter of Indra. Some say, this is a metaphor for the army (sena) of the gods (deva) that he commanded.

His true love was Valli, a tribal girl who wandered in millet fields and would not marry him. He tried to charm her with amorous words but she turned away from him. He took the form of a bangle-seller, then a sage, and tried to endear himself to her. But she drove him away.

So Ganesha took the form of a wild elephant and frightened the girl until she sought refuge in Murugan's arms. Murugan drove

the elephant away and won Valli's heart. Her father opposed their wedding, but Murugan fought him and his sons with his lance. Impressed by his valour they accepted him as son-in-law of the tribe.

- Story of Murugan is popular in Tamil Nadu. In North Indian traditions, he is a bachelor who shuns the company of women and is liked to war and death, hence widows.

- In temples, enshrined male gods often are shown with two consorts, one on either side, both for visual symmetry and for conveying the idea of balance. Devasena refers to the heavens and Valli refers to the earth.

- Ganesha is also portrayed with two wives: Riddhi for material pleasure and Siddhi for spiritual pleasure. Vishnu is portrayed with two wives, one bhoga-patni for sensual pleasure and the other yoga-patni enabling spiritual liberation.

- While Shiva is linked to Gauri, the kitchen goddess, he is sometimes connected with Ganga, the demanding wife who sits on his head. Gauri forces Ganga to leave Kailash and flow in the south as the river Godavari.

- In Maharashtra, the folk-god, Khandoba is the killer of demons, who is married to women from many communities: Mhalsa is from the trading communities, and Banai is from the shepherd community. Then there are wives from the community of tailors, garland-makers and oilpressers. One wife is identified as Muslim too. Thus, the god is seen as uniting diverse communities.

51. Saubhari and His Fifty Wives

Saubhari went to King Mandata and sought one of his fifty daughters as his wife. But the king refused as Saubhari was old and ugly, gaunt by years of austerity in the forest. So, using his magic powers, Saubhari made himself young and handsome. This time when he went to Mandhata, all his fifty daughters desired him as their husband. So, to satisfy all the women equally, Saubhari multiplied himself fifty times. Each of Mandhata's daughters got a husband to her satisfaction.

- This story comes from the Srimad Bhagavatam. It reveals the sexual prowess of a man who gains mastery over his senses.
- Similar stories are told of Krishna. When Narada visits his city, he finds 16,108 palaces for Krishna's 16,108 queens. In each palace there is a Krishna, giving each one total attention. Krishna even multiplies during the raas-leela to satisfy each and every gopika or milkmaid.
- These stories suggest that only a man who can satisfy all his wives equally and fully should marry multiple times.

52. Chandra and the Nakshatras

The moon-god Chandra had married the twenty-seven constellations, or Nakshatra, that circle the sky. But he preferred only one of them, Rohini, and ignored the rest.

His father-in-law, Daksha, warned to give equal attention to all wives or face dire consequences. When he did not listen, Daksha cursed Chandra with the wasting disease. He began to wane with each passing day. To save himself, he prayed to Shiva who placed him on his forehead and enabled him to wane.

Realizing his mistake Chandra gave equal attention to all his wives, one night for each one, waxing when he approached his favourite, Rohini each month and waning when he moved away from her.

- This story comes from the Somnath Sthal Purana.
- The importance given to the satisfaction of the woman is paramount in this story.
- A woman comes to the king's court and declares that the only way women will be faithful to their husbands is if the king trains the husbands to be great lovers. This results in the writing of the Koka Shastra. It is a special book designed for husbands who wish to keep their wives happy, so the wives will remain faithful to them.

53. Siri

After the death of his wife and daughter, Bermanna was consumed by depression and left the affairs of his estate to a distant relative Anna Shetty. Brahmadeva appeared to Bermanna and told him to worship his old family deity if he wished an heir. Bermanna did as advised and to his surprise, in the basket of offerings made to the family deity he found a daughter who he named Siri. She would be the heir of all his estate.

Siri grew up to be a beautiful woman and Kantha Poonja, from the neighbouring village, sought her hand in marriage. His mother secured Siri's hand by assuring the old Bermanna that his son would manage the affairs of her vast estate on Siri's behalf. And so, the wedding was held and Siri moved into her husband's house.

During the baby shower, her husband gifted her a costly sari in keeping with custom. The moment Siri received it she knew that the fabric had been draped on the body of another woman once. She realized her husband had a mistress. She was furious and refused to wear the secondhand garment. Kantha Poonja was thus publicly humiliated and he never forgave Siri.

Siri went to her father's house for the delivery. She gave birth to her son. To her shock, her husband did not come to fetch her back. Soon Bermanna died. Anna Shetty claimed the land as his own and Siri's husband did not fight for her property rights. She

was thus left to fend for herself. Furious, she cursed her husband that his lands would become infertile and his clan would perish. She then proceeded to burn her own house down with her powers and then set out to start a new life. On the way, death claimed her son and her servants.

But she did not give up. She was given shelter by two brothers who accepted her as their sister. And she found a new husband and bore him a daughter. When she died, she became a goddess, a spirit that protects women who are treated badly by their husbands and other guardians.

- This story comes from Tulu Nadu in Karnataka. It is part of oral lore. Siri is worshipped as a guardian spirit (bhuta) especially for women.
- This story forces us to look beyond Brahminical beliefs and customs. Here the woman does not take kindly to her husband having a mistress. She is a woman with property. She leaves her husband, fights for her property, punishes those who cheat her, and eventually marries and finds happiness with another man. It's a story of female agency that is not given mainstream attention and remains restricted to the community.
- Paddanna is a long form poem sung for the divine spirits that guard the Tulu community. One of them refers to seven Jain brothers who had one sister called Muthu; they married her to 24 men but each groom died the night of marriage until she married Muruva Beary, a trader from a distant land. From this union came Bobbariya who

became a great sea traveller and eventually guardian of sea-travellers.

- Tulus in coastal Karnataka have a tale of the origin of the matrilineal form of succession. A bhoota-deva kept destroying ships sailing to Arabia until the king promised to drown a young willing male in his honour. Seven of the king's sons refused but his sister's son agreed. The spirit was pleased with the willingness to sacrifice himself to the community and declared that the nephew, not son, shall be the next king. This was done to please the spirit and save the ships.

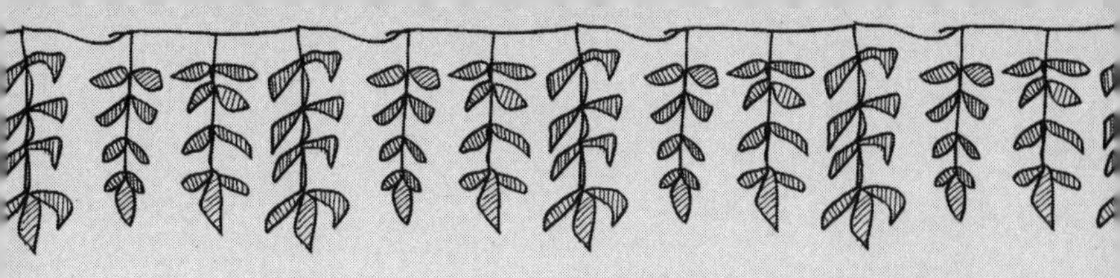

VI

Children

Stories of childless kings are everywhere in Hindu lore. What is the solution then? Another wife, or the invitations to a stranger to come to the wife? Is a child thus conceived to be considered legitimate? Does it matter if a son is birthed by one woman and raised by another? How are family trees traced? Which father is legitimate; which mother is illegitimate?

54. Urvashi's Fathers and Sons

Indra sent damsels called apsaras to tempt the sages Nara and Narayana. They laughed and rubbed their thighs. From that rubbing of the thigh was born Urvashi, more beautiful than all the damsels sent by Indra

Mitra and Varuna shed their semen in pots at the sight of the beautiful Urvashi. From the pot emerged Agastya and Vasishtha. Rishi Vibhandaka also released semen at the sight of Urvashi, which was eaten by a doe who gave birth to a child with antlers.

- Many tales of Urvashi are found in Vedic and Puranic literature.
- Her unusual birth shows how men with great powers can produce children without women.
- In these stories, marriage is separated from childbirth. The gods produce children, but not marry.
- Nara-Narayana and Mitra-Varuna are identified as male pairs, usually seen as teacher-student or brothers or friends or partners. Queer see them as lovers. Which gaze is authentic?

55. Birth of Ganesha and Kartikeya

The gods wanted Shiva to marry Shakti but did not want a child who contained both their powers. So, they interrupted the lovemaking of Shiva and Shakti. Shiva's seed was captured by Agni, the fire-god. But it singed him. So, he gave it to Vayu, the wind-god. But he could not cool it either. He cast it in the river Ganga. The water began to boil and set aflame the forest of reeds on the riverbank. When the fire subsided, six lotus flowers were seen each containing a baby boy. The Kritika constellation of six stars took the form of six nursemaids and fed the children. Shakti saw Shiva's children and merged the six into one and gave the youth a spear with which to fight enemies and protect the weak.

But Shakti wanted a child of her own. Shiva was not interested as he was immortal and had no ancestors to whom debts had to be repaid. Parvati said she needed a child to give her company when Shiva was busy meditating. But Shiva did not think too much of her loneliness. And so, when he went away to meditate the next time, she smeared her body with turmeric and oil and the paste of many plants, and collected the rubbings and molded out of it a doll into which she breathed life. Thus, was born Vinayak, a child created without a father (nayak). Shakti enjoyed his company and did not miss Shiva. He watched over the cave when she went to bathe. That is when Shiva returned and seeing a stranger at Shakti's cave, blocking his entry, became angry. A duel followed and Shiva raised his trident and severed Vinayak's

head. Shakti came out and saw her headless son and began to wail and threatened to destroy everything if he was not resurrected. So, Shiva told his ganas to bring him the head of the first creature they encountered in the northern direction. They came back with the head of an elephant, which was placed on Vinayak's headless body. Vinayak came back to life as Gajanan, the elephant-headed one, and he was appointed Ganesha, the leader of Shiva's ganas.

- Shiva is an ascetic, but a lot of stress is given to his children. Kartikeya is produced without the help of Shakti as many male and female gods serve as surrogate mothers. Ganesha is produced without the help of Shiva, though eventually he contributes. Thus, marriage is separated from childbearing and the sovereignty of Shiva and Shakti is established. Neither is dependent.
- Shiva is a hermit but in images he is often shown with his wife and two children. These were clearly narratives that became popular to challenge the rise of monastic orders. Shiva is god because he marries. Buddha becomes enlightened when he gives up marriage.
- Shiva's autonomy is repeatedly stressed—he does not want children, but his wife does, the gods do.

56. Torn between Brihaspati and Chandra

Tara, the star-goddess, was married to stern Brihaspati, lord of the planet, Jupiter. But she was in love with Chandra, the romantic moon-god. One day, she eloped with her handsome lover. Brihaspati refused to perform yagna for Indra until he brought his wife back. A war took place in the celestial regions between those who supported Tara's husband and those who supported her lover. Finally, for the sake of Indra's yagna, Chandra let Tara go back to Brihaspati.

Tara came back with a child. Brihaspati claimed the child as his own. Chandra insisted it was his. The child inside said that he was fruit of Chandra's seed. This made Brihaspati very angry, and he cursed the child to be born androgynous. That child was Budh, lord of the planet Mercury.

Indra declared that though biologically Budh was the son of Chandra, legally he was the son of Brihaspati, who was Tara's wedded husband, not Chandra.

- This story comes from the Mahabharata.
- Here Mercury's androgyny is the result of a curse and the curse is a result of jealousy between two men fighting over a woman.
- This story reveals the tension between a loveless arranged marriage and a passionate love affair.

57. Narikavacha

Long ago, Haihaiya kings attacked the hermitage of Jamadagni, stole his cow and killed him when he tried to stop them. Furious, Jamadagni's son, Parashurama, raised his axe and proceeded to kill fifty clans of warriors who ruled the earth. The earth was bereft of men belonging to warrior clans, save one, who hid in the women's chambers. He was named Narikavacha, he who took refuge behind women.

The widows of the warriors went to Narikavacha and he gave them a child. This child officially belonged to the dead husbands. Thus their lineage was regenerated, through wives.

- The story is found in oral tradition and many Puranas.
- In other versions of the tale, the kshatriya women go to brahmin men to get children.
- It refers to warrior clans whose menfolk are killed in battle, forcing women to go to other men to ensure continuity of the family tree.
- This story reminds one that Vedic times did not privilege biological fatherhood and valued legal fatherhood. Marriage determined fatherhood, not sex.

58. Yayati's Sons

Shukra was the royal priest at the court of the asura-king Vrishaparva. His daughter, Devayani, and the king's daughter, Sarmishtha, were friends. But one day, while bathing in a river, their clothes got exchanged and the princess accused Devayani of theft, called her father the king's servant, and pushed her in a well.

Yayati, king of Hastinapur, was passing by. He pulled her out. He held her right hand while doing so. That makes you my husband, said Devayani. Yayati knew the rules of marriage and so accepted Devayani as his queen, even though she was daughter of a priest.

Devayani told her father what had happened, and he was furious for he loved his daughter very much. He refused to serve as the king's priest unless the king punished his daughter. Sarmishtha's punishment was to serve as Devayani's maid.

When Devayani went to Hastinapur with her husband, she was accompanied by her maid-princess, Sarmishtha. Yayati was a dutiful husband but he found his wife's maid more attractive, as she had a regal air about her.

In time, Devayani gave birth to a son called Yadu. Later, Sarmishtha gave birth to a son called Puru, but refused to disclose the name of her lover to Devayani. But truth cannot be hidden for long and when Devayani learnt of her husband's affair with Sarmishtha, she

ran to her father's house.

In a fit of rage, Shukra cursed Yayati that he would become old and impotent. But then he realized his daughter would suffer most from such a curse. And so, told the king that his youth and potency would be restored if one of his sons agreed to suffer in his place.

Yadu refused. Puru agreed.

Yayati enjoyed a double youth, thanks to his son. That is the value of marrying and having sons. They take away your suffering.

In gratitude, Yayati made the younger but illegitimate Puru his heir and cursed the older and legitimate Yadu that neither he nor his descendants would have the right to wear a crown. For men, loyalty is more important than legitimacy.

- This story comes from the Mahabharata.
- Here there is tension between brahmin wife and kshatriya wife, between legitimate wife and mistress, between obedient sons and disobedient sons, between elder sons and younger sons.
- Property in Ramayana is passed on to the eldest son, Ram, but in the Mahabharata it is passed on to the favourite son (Puru) and later to the son of the favorite wife (Satyavati's Vichitra).

59. Mamata's Womb

Yayati had a daughter called Madhavi. It was foretold she would bear four sons who would be great kings. One day, a sage called Galava came to Yayati and asked for eight hundred horses for his guru, Vishwamitra.

Yayati had no horses. But greedy for merit he gave Galava his daughter, Mamata. Yayati asked Mamata to offer up her womb that would bear a great son to whomsoever could give him six hundred horses.

Accordingly, Galava offered Mamata to the kings of the earth. Three kings accepted the offer: they begat sons on Mamata, enabling Galava to obtain six hundred more horses. Galava gave these six hundred horses to Vishwamitra. He then offered Vishwamitra the womb of Mamata, to father a son, which would be worth two hundred more horses. Thus, was Galava's fee repaid.

After bearing four sons, Mamata returned to her father. He offered to get her married. But she chose to become an ascetic.

After passing on the crown to Puru, Yayati renounced the world and ascended to Swarga, for he had earned much merit by enabling Galava pay his tuition fees to Vishwamitra. He enjoyed the pleasures of paradise until he exhausted his merit. Then the gods cast him out. To go back, he needed more merit.

So Yayati went to his daughter Madhavi who lived as a hermit

in the forest. Feeling sorry for her father, she went to her four sons, who were now illustrious kings, and requested them to give a quarter of their merits to their grandfather. They hesitated as Yayati had treated Mamata so badly. But Mamata forgave her father and asked her sons to do the same. They reluctantly agreed and enabled Yayati to return to paradise.

- This story comes from the Mahabharata.
- The father uses his daughter, and her sons, to earn merit.
- Here the woman is just a child-bearing machine, not a wife.
- In many communities, the bride's name and surname are changed after marriage to mark her shift from property of father to property of husband.

60. Satyavati, the Mother of Kings

A fisherman found a pair of twins in the belly of a fish, a boy and a girl. The local king took the son but let the fisherman raise the daughter. Rejected by a king, the fisherman's daughter swore to be mother of kings. Her name was Satyavati.

She ferried people across the river. One day, a Rishi named Parasara stopped the ferry midway, on a river island, and asked her to help him father a child and repay his

debt to ancestors. The child when born would be fully grown and her virginity would be restored, he also assured her. She would also become so fragrant that all men would desire her. The conditions seemed fair, and Satyavati agreed and thus became mother of a dark child on the river island who would grow up to be Vyasa, the compiler and organizer of Vedic hymns.

Many men wanted to marry Satyavati. But she only wanted to marry a king. Old king Shantanu was smitten by her beauty. She agreed to marry him provided her son would inherit his kingdom. To this, Shantanu could not agree as he had a son from an earlier marriage.

But that son, to please his father, gave up rights to the throne and even gave up conjugal rights, so that his children would never threaten Satyavati's children. For this sacrifice he became known as Bhisma, the one mighty enough to take a vow that would entrap him in the hell of Put, reserved for the childless, forever.

- This story comes from the Mahabharata.
- It reveals how the only way women could obtain power was through husbands.
- Ram and Bhisma are both obedient sons. But both are not equally respected. Ram is worshipped as god while Bhisma is pinned to the battlefield by Krishna. This is because Ram's obedience does not violate dharma: it reinforces royal integrity when his father, the king's word is kept. Bhisma's obedience violates dharma: it indulges his father, the king's carnal desire at the cost of the kingdom's stability.

61. Sons for Vichitra's Widows

Vichitra had two wives but he died before he could make either of them pregnant. So Satyavati summoned her firstborn, Vyasa, and asked him to make his daughters-in-law pregnant. Legally, the children conceived would be Vichitra's.

Vyasa asked for time to make his body beautiful, worthy of the widows. But Satyavati was impatient. So, Vyasa went immediately to the two queens. Ambika shut her eyes when she saw Vyasa's fierce form, hardened by years of performing austerities in the forest. Ambalika's face paled. And so Ambika bore a blind child who was named Dhritarashtra and Ambalika bore a weak child called Pandu.

They were called the sons of Vichitra, though they sprouted from Vyasa's seed and were raised by Bhisma, Satyavati's stepson.

Disappointed with these two sons, Satyavati wanted Ambika to go to Vyasa again. But Ambika sent her maid. And the maid bore a wonderful son named Vidura. He had all the royal qualities but was not allowed to be king, as he was not deemed legitimate.

- This story comes from the Mahabharata.
- The story explicitly speaks of the practice of 'niyoga'—getting another man to make the wife of a dead or impotent man pregnant. Here marriage is separated from childbirth.

- The power of women gradually declines over generations. Ganga demands freedom in order to get married. Satyavati demands inheritance. Satyavati's daughters-in-law have no freedom over their bodies.

- Here we see how caste matters. A healthy child born of a servant is not worthy of kingship but an unhealthy child born of a princess is considered worthy.

- The Mahabharata tells the story of one Vyushtiashva who dies childless. His widow clings to his corpse and refuses to let it be cremated. Finally, the gods tell her to lie beside the dead body and that makes her pregnant.

- Rig Vedic funeral hymns tell a widow to lie beside her dead husband but is then asked to rise holding the hand of another man and return to the world of the living.

62. Sons for Pandu

Being blind, Dhritarashtra was not allowed to be king. The crown was given to Pandu. Kunti, the Yadava princess, chose Pandu as her husband. But she was deemed unsuitable as there were rumours of her having a child before marriage. Pandu's prowess in the battlefield earned him the respect of Shalya, the king of Madra, who gave his sister in marriage to Pandu. For Dhritarashtra a wife was brought from Gandhara. When she discovered he was blind, she blindfolded herself for life.

Gandhari soon became pregnant. And while she was pregnant,

Dhritarashtra made a maid pregnant too. The maid gave birth to Yuyutsu while Gandhari's pregnancy continued for a long time.

Pandu became insecure. He had two wives but no children. He went out deer hunting and accidentally shot a stag mating with a doe, which turned out to be Rishi Kindama and his wife, who had taken these forms to mate in public. Kindama cursed Pandu that if he touched any woman he would die instantly. Realizing he would never father children, Pandu decided to become a hermit. He sent word to his wives of his decision and passed on the crown to Dhritarashtra.

Kunti and Madri rushed to the forest. On learning of Pandu's curse, Kunti offered a way out. She had been given a magical formula by Rishi Durvasa that would summon any god who would be compelled to give her a child. But she could do that only with her husband's permission.

Pandu asked Kunti to summon Dharma and then Vayu. So, she became mother of Yudhishtira and Bhima. Then Kunti summoned Indra and he gave her Arjuna. Call more gods, said Pandu. But Kunti reminded her that Shvetaketu's law allows a woman to have only four men in their lives. She had exhausted her turns.

Pandu asked the formula be given to Madri and with her first formula she summoned the Ashwin twins who gave her twin sons, Nakul and Sahadev. So Kunti refused to give the formula again

to her co-wife, her husband's favourite, as then she could have borne more sons than her.

Gandhari, meanwhile, frustrated that she had conceived before Kunti but had not delivered yet, beat her pregnant belly with an iron bar. Out came flesh like a ball of iron that Vyasa put into a hundred pots. From these pots were born the hundred Kauravas. An extra piece left was put in a pot so that Gandhari could have the girl-child she desired. Her name was Dushala.

Thus technically, Pandu, through Kunti and Madri, became father of five sons. Technically, he had another son, named Karna, borne by Kunti before marriage, by the grace of the sun-god. Since she was not married then, Kunti did not tell anyone about the child. She cast him away in a basket to a river's whim. He was found and raised by charioteers. He wanted to learn archery but teachers refused as he did not know his lineage. He ended up being befriended by the Kauravas who made him king. And he abused Draupadi for having five husbands, one more than the stipulated four.

- This story comes from the Mahabharata.
- Paternity is a huge issue in the Mahabharata. Pandavas are fathered by gods. They are raised by Bhisma, who is himself not married. But they are considered children of Pandu, simply because he married their mother. The legal father is thus more important than the biological and foster father.
- This story draws attention to the tension between co-wives. The status of women is dependent on the number of children they bear. Kunti does not want Madri to have more children than her. The Mahabharata thus captures

the competitive nature of women in a household who fight battles through their children.

- In Puranas, Kashyapa's wife Kadru, mother of serpents, has more children than Vinata's two and so is proud but Vinata's children, the birds, turn out to be more powerful.
- Some people said Krishna was of royal blood, his mother was Devaki, sister of Kansa, daughter of Ugrasena, and his father was Vasudeva, son of Surasena. But others said he was a cowherd, raised as he was by Nanda and his wife, Yashoda. Parentage prevented him from being seen as king. As cowherd, he could not be king. And as Vasudeva's son, hence of Yadava lineage, he was not allowed to be king, because of Yayati's curse. Thus, marriage decides the destiny of children. Krishna chose to be a charioteer and is worshipped as cowherd, but never as king.
- In Jain literature, Mahavira is conceived in a brahmin woman's body and the embryo is transferred to a more worthy womb, the body of queen. Similarly, in Bhagavata, Balarama is conceived by Devaki, Vasudeva's wife who like him is a Yadava, but the embryo is transferred to the womb of Rohini, Vasudeva's other wife, who is a cowherd. This creates confusion about lineage and hence status.

63. Shakuntala

Kanva found a girl abandoned on the forest floor and raised her as his own child. He named her Shakuntala. When Shakuntala was a young girl, a king came to their hermitage. He was hunting deer and had lost his way. His name was Dushyant.

Kanva was away on a pilgrimage and so Shakuntala took care of the guest. She fell in love with him and he made love to her passionately. But then it was time for him to go.

A few weeks later, she discovered she was pregnant. Kanva was overjoyed. Shakuntala waited for Dushyant to return, as promised, to take her to his palace. He never came.

A son was born. He was named Bharat, strong enough to wrestle lions. The son wanted to meet his father and so Shakuntala took him to Dushyant's palace. But Dushyant did not recognize her. Was he pretending? Or had he really forgotten? He accused Shakuntala of lying. Who witnessed our marriage, he asked? And she said, the trees, the wind, the earth, the deer, the sun and the moon. Everyone laughed.

The devas got angry and caused a terrible disease to claim all of Dushyant's sons by his other wives. Left without an heir, Dushyant had no choice but to acknowledge Shakuntala as his queen and Bharat as his heir.

- This story is found in the Mahabharata and is a famous poem by Kalidasa. In the Mahabharata, the child is born in the hermitage and Shakuntala only goes to Dushyanta as her son wants to meet his father. In the Kalidasa poem, composed about 1000 years later, she is taken when she is pregnant to her husband, so that no one dishonours her. In Kalidasa a curse is used as a narrative tool to explain Dushyanta's behaviour.

- Shakuntala's son Bharat is said to be the king whose children establish Bharat-varsha, the land of Bharatas, i.e., India.
- The story speaks of the importance of heirs and how illegitimate heirs became important when the legitimate ones die. It draws attention to how marriage changes the status of a woman and her child.
- Kanva is a single father who adopts a girl-child.

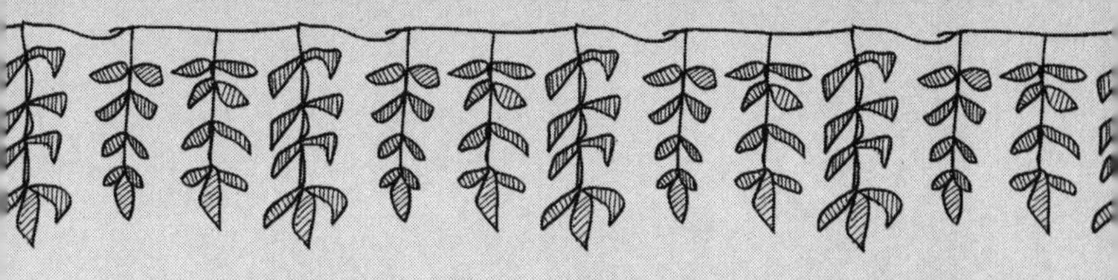

VII

Property

Folk epics inform us of wars fought over generations over land, cattle and bruised egos. It is only because you know who your father is, that you are able to carry forward property disputes and vendetta.

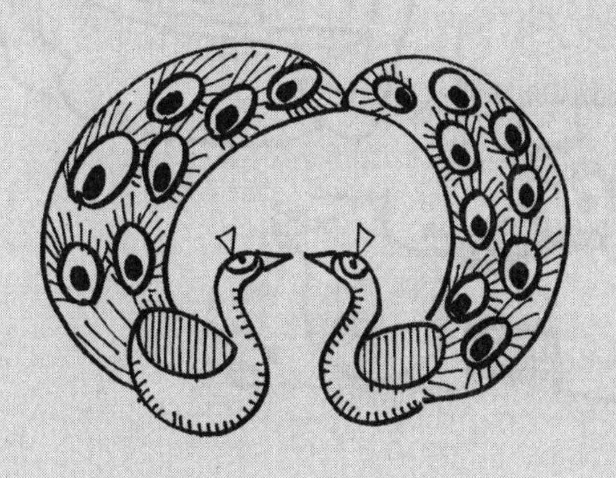

64. Sachi Makes Indra Nervous

Indra, king of devas, lives in a paradise called Swarga. One day, a handsome resplendent man came into his hall, and Indra saw Sachi leave his side and walk beside this new entrant. And everyone bowed to this new entrant and declared him to be the ruler of Swarga, master of all its splendours.

Indra was furious. His wife had been unfaithful, choosing another man over him.

Sachi clarified, 'He who performs most yagnas becomes Indra. If someone performs more yagnas than you, then he becomes Indra and I become his wife. Only the one who has the greatest number of yagnas is worthy of Swarga and Sachi. We belong to no one but the worthiest performer of the maximum number of yagnas.'

Such is the marriage of Indra and Sachi. She makes him insecure as she is not faithful to him. She is faithful to the position he occupies.

- This theme is part of Hindu and Buddhist folklore.
- The Vedic Indra lost his exalted position in later Indian literature and was seen as replaceable. His throne and kingdom were visualized as a woman, Sachi, a form of Lakshmi, who is faithful to the position, not the man. She therefore constantly seeks a worthier groom.
- The bride is often equated with Lakshmi, the goddess of fortune, who is described as chanchal (fickle). Her arrival is shubh and mangal: it ushers in happiness and prosperity. She gives husband access to her wealth and to her father's wealth. But the groom is told to be vigilant (savdhaan). Is it because the bride is Lakshmi, whimsical, and can reject him for a worthier man? Or because the good fortune may enchant him and destroy his good sense?

65. Remarriage of Tara

The monkey-king Riksha had fallen into an enchanted lake and had emerged with a female body. The rain-god found him attractive and gave him/her a son called Vali. The sun-god also found him attractive and gave him/her a son called Sugriva. Thus, Riksha had two sons who called him father and mother. Vali, the older one, married the beautiful Tara. Sugriva, the younger one, married Ruma.

When Riksha was dying, he told Vali and Sugriva to share the kingdom of Kishkinda and be its joint rulers. But a misunderstanding split the brothers. Vali drove Sugriva out of Kishkinda and claimed the foraging grounds for himself. He also claimed Ruma as his wife.

When Ram killed Vali, Sugriva became king of Kishkinda. He reaffirmed his authority by marrying Vali's queen, Tara, the wise one.

- This story is from the Ramayana.
- Ruma plays no significant role other than establishing Vali as villain but marriage to Tara is clearly linked to kingship.
- When Ram killed Ravana, and made Vibhishana king of Lanka, Vibhishana reaffirmed his authority by marrying Ravana's queen, Mandodari.
- Remarriage being part of the Ramayana is not popular discourse perhaps as Tara and Mandodari are seen as belonging to 'low', 'unrefined', groups such as vanaras and rakshasas.

66. Hidimba, Who Was Not Good Enough

The hundred Kauravas hated their cousins, the five, very talented, Pandava brothers. So, they gifted them a palace made of lac and cloth and set it aflame while they were asleep. But the Pandavas managed to escape through a tunnel to the forest.

In the forest, Bhima, the mightiest of Pandavas, battled many rakshasas—Baka, Jata, Hidimbh. Impressed by his strength,

desirous of peace, Hidimbh's sister, Hidimba, offered to marry Bhima and take care of his mother and his brothers, feeding them and protecting them. Bhima agreed and so Hidimba became his wife and bore him a son called Ghatotkacha.

But Hidimba's mother-in-law, Kunti, saw her as a wild forest woman and did not think of her as a legitimate daughter-in-law. She encouraged her sons to leave Hidimba's lair, return to civilization and find a way to secure their inheritance.

- This story comes from the Mahabharata.
- Both the Ramayana and the Mahabharata deal with kingship. Kings exist to prevent property disputes that lead to anarchy.
- The two epics distinguish the settled realms of Arya from the forest abodes of rakshasas and vanaras.
- In both epics, the women are identified by the land they belong to indicating how their value comes from the kinship ties. There is Kaushalya of Kaushala-desha, Kaikeyi of Kekeya-desha, Madri of Madra-desha, and Gandhari of Gandhara-desha.

67. Revati and Balarama

Kakudmi went, along with his daughter, Revati, to meet Brahma, seeking his advice on a worthy groom for her. Unfortunately, a day at Brahma's is a thousand years on earth. By the time father and daughter returned, the world had forgotten them. The world had also shrunk in size. No one now wanted to marry Revati as she was too tall.

But then Krishna came with his elder brother Balarama to their island-kingdom of Dwarka. They were looking for a home after their city Mathura had been burnt to the ground by Jarasandha. Everyone was afraid of the giant man and his daughter. But not Balarama who swung his plough, hooked it on Revati's shoulder to make her bend, so he could see her better. As soon as the plough touched her shoulder, Revati shrunk in size.

Kakudmi was pleased and offered Revati's hand in marriage to Balarama, and invited his family to stay on the island, and consider it their own.

- This story comes from folklore based on Bhagavata and it links Dwarka to Revati. By marrying her, the Yadavas get a home, just as in the forest Pandavas get a home when Bhima marries Hidimba.
- When the boy's family approaches the girl's family, it is called the way of Prajapati.

- When the girl's family approaches the boy's family, it is called the way of Brahma.
- In Prajapati's way, since the girl is given to help the boy repay his debt to ancestors, without seeking anything in return, the rite is called 'kanya-daan' (daughter-charity). It gives great merit to the girl's father.
- In Brahma's way, the bride is made more desirable by the promise of many gifts. This may be the origin of dowry.

68. Satya's Marriage

Nagnajit, king of Kosala, invited warriors from all over the land to tame seven of his wildest bulls and win his daughter Satya's hand in marriage. Kings came, tried and failed. Finally, Krishna, scion of the Yadava clan, entered the ring.

He multiplied his body seven times. With each form, he grabbed a bull by the horns and forced it into submission. Krishna then tied the seven bulls with a rope and dragged them towards Nagnajit as if they were seven toy bulls.

Pleased with this display of courage and strength, Nagnajit was more than happy to let Satya marry Krishna.

- This story comes from the Bhagavata Purana.
- Here the daughter is a trophy to be won by proving one's capability in a tournament. This is how Arjuna marries Draupadi and Ram marries Sita.

- Jarasandha burns Mathura and Krishna finds refuge on the island of Dwarka. But his marriages create important political alliances as his many wives are princesses from powerful kingdoms: Satya is from Kosala, Bhadra from Kekeya, Lakshman from Madra, Mitravinda from Avanti, Nagnajit from Kosala, Rukmini from Vidarbha. Thus, marriages enable political alliances.

69. A Kingdom for Draupadi

Drupada declared that whosoever could strike the eye of a fish looking at its reflection below would marry his daughter. He hoped this would get him Arjuna, the greatest archer in the world, as his son-in-law, but news reached him that Arjuna and his four brothers, had been killed by their cousins, the Kauravas, in a palace fire.

The tournament was thrown upon to all kings. Karna, king of Anga, came forward but Draupadi rejected him as he was not a real king. His kingdom was but a gift bestowed upon him by the Kauravas. Besides Karna, was raised by charioteers and did not know who his real parents were. A man without lineage was not worthy of her.

The tournament was thrown upon to sages who live in the forest, some of whom were archers. One such sage-archer came forward and managed to do the impossible feat. He took Draupadi with him to his mother. The mother on learning that her son had won an archery tournament asked him to share the

gift won with his four brothers. And so Draupadi was shared by five brothers. She realized, they were none other than the Pandava brothers, hiding in the forest, after the assault on their lives.

With Draupadi as wife, and Drupada as father-in-law, the Pandavas bravely presented themselves at Hastinapur and asked their cousins, Kauravas, for their share of property. The Kauravas had no choice but to divide their land and give them the forest of Khandava, on which the Pandavas built their city of Indraprastha.

Pandavas agreed that every brother would spend a year with Draupadi. In that year, she would be his wife and the other brothers' sister-in-law. With this arrangement, Draupadi became the mother of five sons, the Upa-Pandavas.

- This story comes from the Mahabharata.
- The Pandava fortune changes after they marry Draupadi. Draupadi is also responsible for breaking the Kuru household. This is how traditionally daughters-in-law are seen: bringing in fortune and dividing the household.
- Draupadi demands that no other wife of the Pandavas be allowed to enter their place at Indraprastha. The epic accepts both polyandry and polygamy.

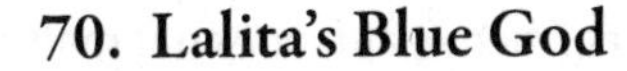

70. Lalita's Blue God

King Indradyumna had heard that a forest tribe had access to a beautiful image of Krishna called Nila Madhav. He ordered his minister, Vidyapati, to fetch it for him by hook or by crook. Vidyapati learnt two things: only the head of the tribe knew the location of the image, and that he had a daughter called Lalita who he loved very much.

Vidyapati wooed Lalita who fell in love with him. As dowry, he asked that he be shown the Nila Madhav image. His father-in-law agreed but took him to the shrine blindfolded. It was a cave deep in the forest. But Vidyapati was clever. He dropped mustard seeds on the forest floor that germinated in the rainy season and gave rise to bright yellow flowers in the autumn.

Vidyapati followed the trail of the flowers, alone, and found the cave and tried to steal the image of Nila Madhav. That is when there was a terrible storm of rain and dust. It covered the mouth of the cave. Nila Madhav was lost forever because of Indradyumna's cupidity and Vidyapati's false marriage.

- The story comes from the temple lore of Jagannath, in Puri, Odisha.
- Vidyapati marries Lalita not because he cares for her, but because he wants access to something through her. What she has is more important than who she is. The gods do not approve of that.
- In Krishna lore, Satyabhama thinks that she has more rights on Krishna because she comes with estate and titles. But

she learns that all her wealth does not matter to Krishna as much as the love of Rukmini, symbolized by the tulsi sprig. Property makes marriage comfortable but cannot be the foundation of a relationship.

71. The Brothers' Land

During a famine, Kolatta served a Chola king, and brought prosperity to his barren lands, for which he was gifted land. His eight younger brothers are given land too, but smaller portions, so they hate the elder brother. Some artisans claim that the land belongs to them and this makes them enemies of the Kolatta's family.

Kolatta gets married but does not have children and so his brothers try various schemes to take over his land. Kolatta adopts a child, Kunnutaiya, in his old age but dies soon after. The orphan lad is driven out by his uncles who claim his property.

Kunnutaiya goes through many adventures and finally manages to marry Tamarai. With her by his side, and the intervention of the Chola king, he reclaims his land, much to the irritation of his cousins. But the land remains infertile, and his wife remains barren, until the couple has a dream. They are suffering, as their father did, because he had accidentally killed three cows.

To restore fertility of land and womb, Tamarai performs austerities at the gates of

Mount Kailash: seven years for each cow. After twenty-one years, the fertility of land and womb is restored. Tamarai is pregnant with triplets. But the cousins send a midwife to kill any male child she may deliver. Vishnu intervenes, cuts open her belly, and whisks away Kunnutaiya's twin sons, Ponnar and Shankar, and lets the daughter, Arukkanni, be born in the normal way. The boys are raised by the family goddess, who feeds them tiger's milk, and they grow up faster than their sister.

The sons return and claim their land. They fight the rivals, and even fight the Chola king when he demands excessive taxes. Their power comes from their virgin sister, and their virgin wives, who they never see or touch. All three are locked in palaces, performing sacred rituals, like chaste ascetic women. Their power also comes from a horse, Nila, born on the same day as they were, by the blessings of their mother, and their servant Champuka.

The sister, longing for companionship, seeks a parrot which takes the brothers into the forest and results in a fight with tribals, who in turn send a wild boar to destroy their fields. A war follows. In this war, they win, but many followers are defeated. Filled with remorse, realizing their sixteen years on earth are up, the two brothers kill themselves. Their virgin sister sets aflame the palace where her virgin sisters-in-law are locked up and then immolates herself.

- The 'Brothers' tale' is a Tamil folk epic which is about 500 years old. It is an oral ballad, with many local variations. It belongs to the local land-owning castes, and reveals the tensions linked to ownership.

- Marriage plays a key role. A good wife ensures fertility of the land, grants protection and produces heirs who inherit the property. Here sexuality and violence are closely linked.
- The epic grants itself mainstream legitimacy by declaring the brothers and their sister are Pandavas and Draupadi reborn, and by showing how Shiva, Vishnu and Devi help the heroes realize their grand destiny.
- The connection with the Mahabharata is evident: Pandu dies in the forest but his widow, Kunti, returns to Hastinapur with five sons and claims her husband's kingdom as their inheritance.
- Epics involving three generations of one family fighting over land is found across South India such as ***Epic of Palnadu***, in Andhra Pradesh, and the ***Ballad of Junjappa*** in Karnataka. In all these stories, wives play a crucial role, supporting husbands, and giving them heirs. This parallels struggles over land and cattle.
- Similar epics of violence and marriage are found in North India, in Rajput lands. In Bundelkhand epic Alha, kingdoms that are related by marriage are constantly at war with each other over territory and pride. Prithviraj does not let his daughter Bena go to her husband's house simply because he is accompanied by Alha and Udal, who are considered of 'lower' caste as their mother herded cattle. Eventually, a battle ensues, and Bena's husband Brahma is killed, and Bena becomes his 'sati'.
- Rajasthan and Deccan, are full of tales of men who were

killed protecting land and cattle. They are called 'virs' and often worshipped as gods. Their widows who die on their husband's funeral pyre, dressed as brides, are venerated as 'sati'.

- Fear of widows claiming property is the reason why they were not allowed to remarry, why they were encouraged to perform 'sati' and kill themselves on their husbands' funeral pyre, and why they were cast away in pilgrim spots like Kashi and Mathura, to live as ascetics, with no access to men or income or land.

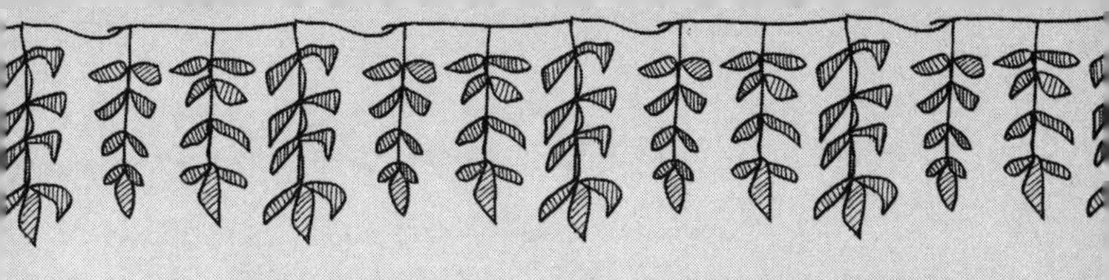

VIII

Barriers

Soul has no gender, said Sulabha, the nun, to King Janaka, in the Mahabharata. If marriage is between souls, then do body, caste, class, gender matter? Yet there are many barriers to the union of souls. Cultural binaries and social boundaries struggle to accommodate nature's fluidity and diversity.

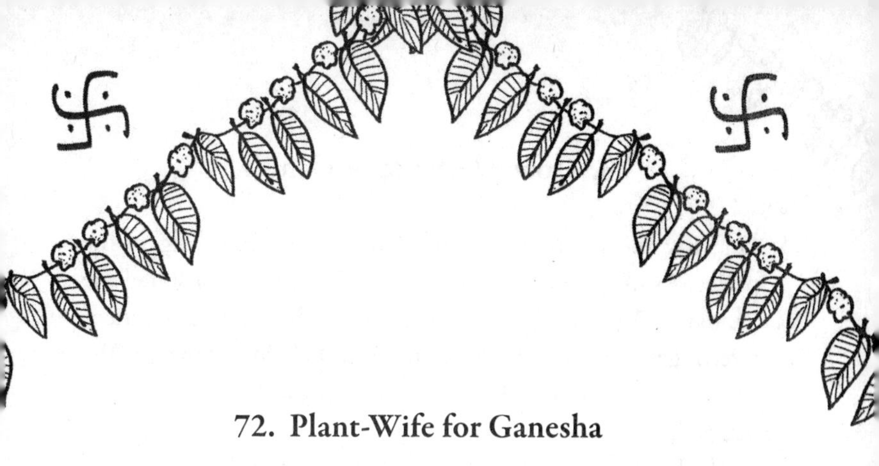

72. Plant-Wife for Ganesha

Some say Ganesha has no wives. Some say he has two, Riddhi and Siddhi, metaphors for material and spiritual success. Some say he has one wife, a Tantric shakti, who sits on his left lap and holds his trunk.

In Bengal they say, no one wanted to marry a boy with an elephant's head. So, his mother gave him a banana plant wrapped in a sari. This is your wife, she said.

- Kola-bau, or the banana wife of Ganesha, is found in every Durga pandal in Bengal.
- Beautiful women clinging to plants are ancient fertility symbols even found in Buddhist shrines.
- In Krishna stories, when a tree is uprooted, gandharvas emerge from it, reminding us of the ancient belief that yakshas and gandharvas live inside trees.

73. Goat-Husband of Gandhari

One day the Kauravas and the Pandavas were playing in the palace. As usual, they began to fight. The Kauravas insulted the Pandavas, 'Your mother was not a virgin when she got married,' referring to rumours that Kunti had a child before marriage. The Pandavas shouted back, 'Your mother was a widow when she got married.'

The Kauravas were shocked to hear this. On investigation, they learnt that astrologers had foretold that Gandhari would become a widow soon after marriage. But her second marriage would be to a great king. To expedite this, she was married to a goat that was killed after which she was given in marriage to Dhritarashtra. The dying goat had cursed her which is why her pregnancy took so long, and her children eventually had to be incubated in pots.

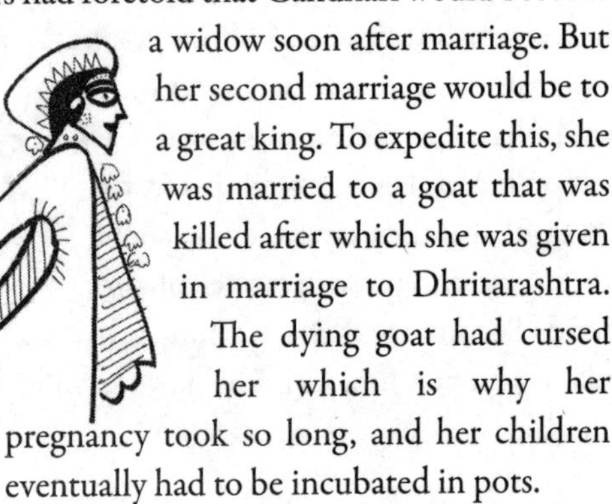

- This story comes from the Telugu Mahabharata and is not part of the mainstream Sanskrit canon.
- In Hindu astrology, women who are said to be 'manglik' with a negative influence of the planet Mars are advised to first marry a tree before marrying a human so that the plant suffers instead of the human husband.

74. Donkey-Father of Bhartrihari

A potter found a donkey in the forest and brought him home, but the donkey insisted he wanted to marry the local princess. He made such a racket that the potter took the donkey to the king and the donkey threatened to destroy the kingdom by striking his hooves to the ground repeatedly, if the king did not give him his daughter as his bride.

So, the king got this daughter married to the donkey. At night, the donkey turned into a god. He told the princess that he had been cursed to turn into a donkey, for embracing one of Indra's apsaras. He made love to the princess and she gave birth to two sons, Vikramaditya and Bhartrihari, who would grow up to be great kings.

When the queen learnt that her daughter had given birth to two sons, she suspected she was being unfaithful to her donkey husband. She spied on her daughter and learnt the donkey's secret. To ensure the god does not become a donkey again, she decided to burn the donkey's skin. She did not realize that by doing so she lifted the curse, and the god was able to return to Indra's paradise, leaving his wife on earth to take care of her children on her own.

- This is an oral epic popular in North India. It is a part of the many tales linked to the legendary brothers in the kingdom of Ujjain.
- The Panchatantra speaks of a childless man who adopts a snake and gets it married to a human woman. The snake eventually turns out to be a god cursed.

75. God-Spouse

A temple priest had no child. So, one day he found a girl-child amongst the tulsi plants in the temple garden and adopted her as his own. She grew up to be a beautiful and talented girl, who would make garlands for the deity with her father.

But one day, her father discovered her hair in a garland. When he demanded an explanation she said, 'I wear them around my neck before I put them around his neck.' Her father said that this was not right.

However, the next day, every garland placed around the deity's neck kept falling down. In a dream, the deity appeared and told his priest that he preferred the garlands adorned with his daughter's hair. She loved him truly and that made the flowers more fragrant.

The temple was once raided by a Muslim sultan and the images of the deity taken to Delhi. Temple priests followed the soldiers and managed to get the image back. Unfortunately for them the sultan's daughter had fallen in love with the image and followed the temple priests. Though she belonged to Turuku dharma, the temple priests accepted her love and established a shrine in her honour. And to show his love for the Muslim princess, the deity is dressed in Muslim attire and eats bread on certain days.

- These are Tamil temple lore of Srivilliputur and Srirangam related to Andal and Bibi Nachyar who are both considered god-wives.
- The priest is Perilavar and his daughter is Godai or Andal. Both are Alvars, renowned for their devotion to Vishnu, known in the south as Perumal.
- In these temples, there are shrines dedicated to the deity's human wives. Andal is a historical figure from eighth century but Bibi Nachyar is probably not. Her story may have emerged around fourteenth century following raids on Southern temples by Delhi sultans.
- In many temples across India from Puri in Odisha to Chidambaram in Tamil Nadu, there were singers and dancers dedicated to the deity who were known by various names including 'devadasi'. They were seen as wives and servants of the gods. This practice was stopped by law in the British era. Women, who never had husbands, were now expected to have husbands, if they wished to be seen as respectable. From being independent performers, with their own income, they became dependent on husbands.

76. Vararuchi's Many Children

Vararuchi was one of the nine jewels in the court of Vikramaditya who believed man makes his own destiny; there is no such thing as fate. One day, he heard birds talking outside his house that he was destined to marry a woman from a community of leather workers and scavengers and corpse-disposers. Vararuchi, an aristocrat, did everything in his power to avoid this, but ended up falling in love, and marrying precisely such a woman. He realized one cannot fight destiny.

Vararuchi and his wife decided to go on a pilgrimage. During the journey she became pregnant several times. Each time she delivered a child, he would ask, 'Does the child have a mouth?' She said yes. 'Then leave it on the forest floor under a tree. If the child is fated to survive, it will survive. Else it will not.' In this way, he made his wife abandon eleven children. The twelfth had no mouth. That child could neither eat food nor cry out for help. It would surely die. But the child did not die, instead it became a deity atop a hill.

The other eleven children were adopted by members of different castes: priests, soldiers, traders, philosophers, washermen, musicians, herdsmen, farmers, architects. Each child was exceptional, a prodigy. Was it because of the high-caste father, the low-caste mother, or the parents of different communities who raised them? No one knew.

- This comes from a popular folk tale in Kerala: 'Parayi Petta Panthirukulam'
- Caste is a major barrier to marriage. Yet this story written around seventeenth century Kerala seeks to challenge

assumptions. Every exceptional child has biological inputs from the highest and lowest castes, and cultural inputs from a third caste.

- Indian philosophy speaks of caste being determined by karma, and marriages being fixed by karma and yet seeks to challenge karma by forcing marriage within caste using roti-beti (daughter-bread) concept which does not allow sharing of vocation, food and daughters outside the community.

77. Samba's Marriage

Samba, son of Krishna and Jambavati, looked just like his father and taking advantage of his looks entered his father's palace and duped his junior queens. For this crime, Krishna cursed his son with skin disease so that he could be distinguished from his father. Samba apologized for his action and was eventually cured by the grace of Surya, the sun-god.

Samba fell in love with Duryodhana's daughter, Lakshmana, and tried to abduct her from her father's house in Hastinapur. But he failed and was thrown in prison by Duryodhana.

The Yadavas came to the rescue of their prince and begged

Duryodhana to release the boy but Duryodhana refused. He was angry with the Yadavas. They had let Balarama's sister marry Arjuna not him. They had let Balarama's daughter marry Arjuna's son not his. He would not let Krishna's son claim his daughter. He insulted the Yadavas and refused to let Samba go.

Balarama, known for his quick temper, did not appreciate Duryodhana's decision. He grew in size and in his gigantic form hooked his plough on the foundations of Hastinapur and threatened to drag it to the sea. Terrified of his power, Duryodhana agreed to let Samba return to Dwarka with Lakshmana as his bride.

- This story comes from the Bhagavata Purana and the Harivamsa.
- Samba crosses the line when he tries to dupe Krishna's wife and is punished for it.
- Samba's behaviour is attributed to his mother being a bear (Jambavati) so probably tribal. Also, he is born by the grace of Shiva who appears in the form of half-woman (sa-Amba, or together with his spouse) and so the child's manners are unpredictable and unrefined and innocent like Shiva.
- Violent opposition of families and clans to marriages is a common theme in mythology. In the Old Testament of the Bible, we find the sons of Jacob killing the man who wants to marry their sister, Diane, even after he undergoes the rite of circumcision for her sake.

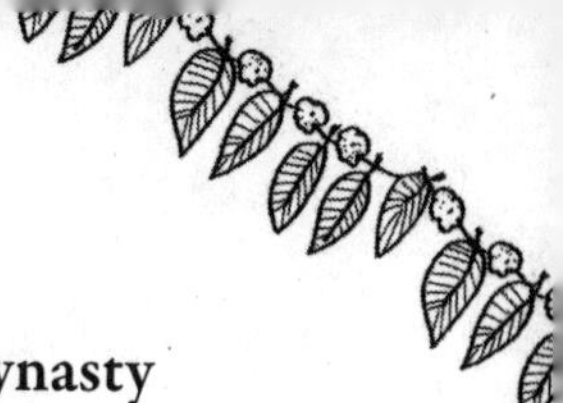

78. The Origins of the Lunar Dynasty

Manu's son, Sudyumna entered an enchanted grove where he turned into a woman called Ila. It was the will of Shakti that only women should exist in that grove, so that no man disturbs her making love with Shiva. Ila begged the divine couple to grant his masculinity back. All they could do was ensure that his masculinity waxed and waned with the moon so that on new moon nights, he was a woman, and on full moon nights he was a man.

Budh, lord of planet mercury, son of the moon-god, adopted son of Jupiter, was cursed to be androgynous. He fell in love with Sudyumna-Ila and their children went on to establish the lunar dynasty of kings, just as Ila's brother, Ikshavaku, had established the solar dynasty of kings.

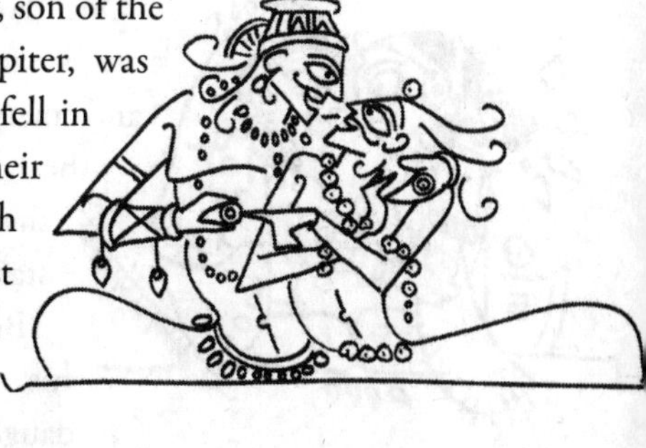

- This story comes from the Mahabharata and many Puranas.
- Why would such a story be told? Why is the origin of lunar dynasty of kings linked to the androgynous and the queer?
- The idea of a forest where men turn into women recurs in classical as well as folk lore.

79. Teeja-Beeja Get Married

Two friends, who lived in distant villages, met at a fair and realized their respective wives were pregnant. They decided to get the unborn children married as the local astrologers predicted their union would bring great happiness.

Both women gave birth to daughters. Both parents assumed the other had given birth to a son. The two girls, Teeja and Beeja, therefore grew up in different villages, each one waiting for her husband.

One day, the girl named Beeja fell in a water talk in the temple of the goddess, and emerged male. The bitch that fell into the water came out a dog. The mare that fell into the water came out a stallion.

Beeja's father sent word to inform his friend of the situation. 'My daughter is now a son. How can he then be bride of your son?' And his friend replied, 'I have no son only a daughter called Teeja. I have been waiting all these years for Beeja, my son-in-law, to come home and fetch her. Send him quickly.'

Thus, Teeja and Beeja got married.

- The story of Teeja and Beeja comes from oral folklore of Rajasthan.
- Many temples in Rajasthan claim to have ponds that change the gender of animals and humans. They reveal an

awareness of queer genders and sexuality.

- Stories of children being promised in marriage before they were even born was an old tribal custom. The married children would come together only when they were mature enough and of child-bearing age. The second wedding after maturity was called 'gauna'.

- In Bengal Baul poetry, Krishna is Kali and Shiva is Radha. Thus, the male becomes female. The one on top becomes the one below. Gender shifts like positions. It is all fluid.

80. Sumedha's Same-Sex-Spouse

Somavat and Sumedha were friends. They learnt that queen Simantini gave cows to new married couples. So, Somavat disguised himself as a woman and went to her palace pretending to be the bride of Sumedha.

Simantini was a devotee of Shiva. So great was her devotion and the power of bhakti that her will always came true. When she gave the cows to Sumedha and Somavat, she blessed them as man and wife. And so, what she willed came true. Somavat became a woman called Somavati and he married Sumedha, once his friend, now her husband.

- The story of Somavat and Sumedha is found in Skanda Purana and many regional retellings.
- We can speculate if this gender change is real or metaphorical. Was same-sex desire expressed through tales of gender change?
- The story draws attention to newlyweds being seen as positive energy and good luck.

81. A Wife for Aravan

During the war at Kurukshetra, Pandavas realized that victory would elude them unless they sacrificed a man with thirty-two auspicious marks. Krishna, Arjun and Aravan (Arjun's son by Uloopi) had such marks. Arjun and Krishna were considered indispensable. Aravan agreed to the sacrifice, provided he was given a wife before the sacrifice. He did not want to die a virgin. And he wanted someone to weep for him when he was gone.

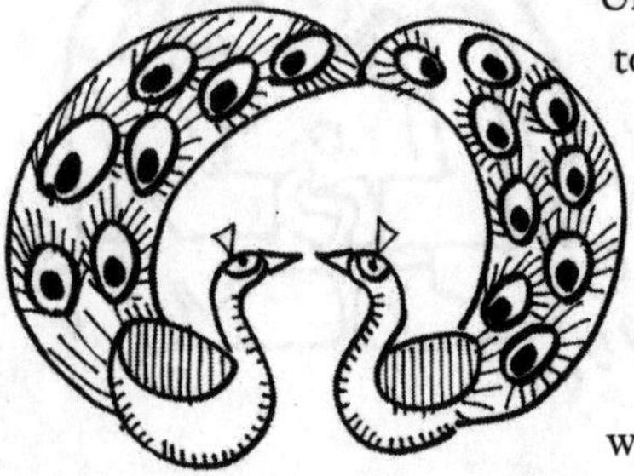

Unfortunately, no woman was willing to marry a man destined to be beheaded at dawn. All eyes turned to Krishna, who took the form of Mohini and became Aravan's bride for one night. They spent the night together and at dawn, when Aravan was beheaded, Krishna wailed for him as no widow ever had.

- This story comes from the Tamil Mahabharata.
- Krishna's androgyny is well known. As Mohini, he enchants Shiva as well as the asuras.
- In temples, Krishna is often visualized as a woman, a form he took to gain access to the women's quarters to disarm his lovers. This is called sakhi-vesh.
- Aravan is considered a form of Shiva, who is also known to be comfortable with androgyny. He is half woman. In Vrindavan, temples of Shiva visualize him as a milkmaid, and he is called Gopeshwar and bedecked as a woman.
- Aravan is worshipped by Tamil transgender community. They see themselves as his bride, androgynous as Mohini.
- The motif of two peacocks dancing, found in medieval art, refers to same-sex union but this is lost on most viewers.

82. Shikhandi's Wife

Hiranyavarna's daughter was given in marriage to Shikhandi, eldest son of Drupada. But on her wedding night she realized that her husband, who behaved like a man, had the genitals of a woman. Furious, she returned to her father's house and accused Drupada of cheating her. Hiranyavarna raised an army and threatened to invade and destroy the kingdom of Panchala.

Shikhandi did not know what to do. He tried to kill himself but was rescued by a yaksha called Sthunakarna who lent Shikhandi his manhood for a night. With the yaksha's manhood, Shikhandi made love to courtesans sent by Hiranyavarna to prove his masculinity. Hiranyavarna apologized for his outburst, forced his daughter to return to her husband, and returned home with his army.

As luck would have it, Kubera, king of yakshas, did not approve of Sthunakarna lending his manhood to Shikhandi. He cursed Sthunakarna that his manhood would return to him only when Shikhandi died. And so Shikhandi, born a woman, lived the rest of his life as man, serving his wife, the princess of Dasharni, who had no reason to complain again.

- This story comes from the Mahabharata.
- Shikhandi is probably a female to male transgendered person.
- Why would the epics tell a story such as this unless the storytellers were familiar with non-binary people? Shikhandi is a pivotal character in the epic, who enables the defeat of Bhisma. Bhisma refuses to see Shikhandi as a man, and insists he is a woman, and so does not raise his bow to fight, enabling Arjuna to pin him to the ground with arrows. The arguments mirror contemporary arguments related to transgenders: are they real men, or women, have they transitioned? Who decides the gender?

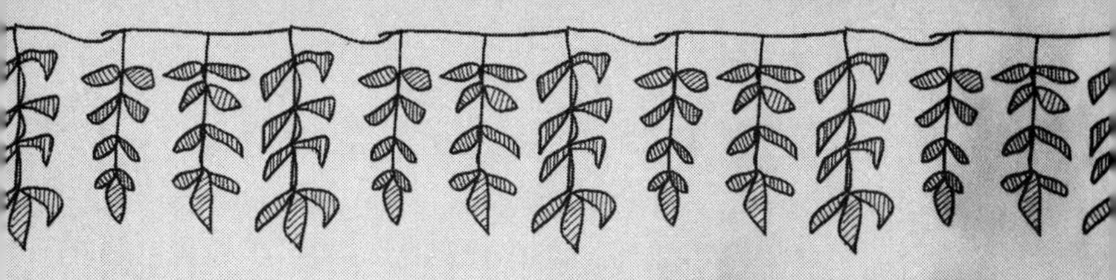

IX

Heartbreak

Sometimes marriages are not meant to happen. One spouse does not consent. Or circumstances conspire to separate a committed couple. The heart breaks. And songs of yearning are composed, begging the wandering jogi to return home.

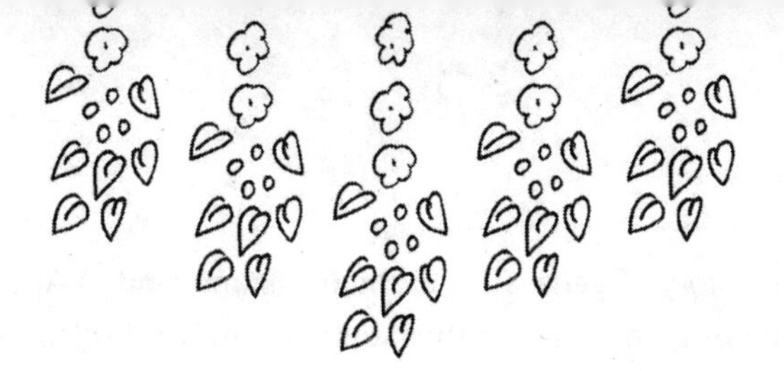

83. Vedavati Waits for Ram

Vedavati wanted to marry Ram so went to the forest to perform austerities until Ram came to her. Ravana wanted to marry her but she jumped into fire to escape. Bhairava asked her to marry him, but she beheaded him. When Ram finally came, he told that he could not marry her for he was ekam-patni-vrata, devoted to his single wife, Sita. But he promised her that he would marry her when he would descend on earth as Tirupati Balaji and she would be reborn as Padmavati.

Many other women wanted to marry Ram. Men too. The sages of the forest were so smitten by his beauty that they wished they were women who could entice him. Ram politely reminded them that he was ekam-patni-vrata. But he assured the heartbroken sages that in his next life, when he would be Krishna, the cowherd, they would be reborn as milkmaids and together they would dance at night in the forest of Madhuvan.

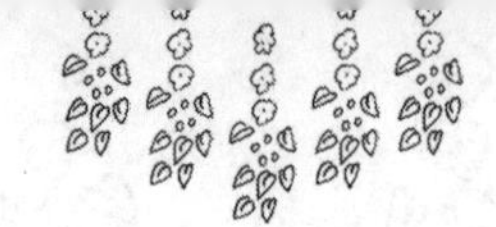

- The story of Vedavati is found in Jammu, and in Andhra Pradesh. In Jammu, the story serves to explain the presence of Vaishnav devi, who kills Bhairav but also orders his worship by her devotees. In Andhra Pradesh, the story serves to explain the marriage of Tirupati Balaji and Padmavati.
- The story of sages falling in love with Ram and wanting to be women comes from the Odia Ramayana retellings.
- Of all Hindu gods, Ram alone is considered ekam-patni-vrata, true to one wife, which makes it ironical when he abandons Sita in the end.

84. Pabuji's Half Wedding

Neither Surpanakha nor her brother Ravana respected the laws of marriage, or the idea of consent.

Surpanakha fell in love with Ram but when he refused, she tried to kill Sita in the hope that with her gone, Ram would agree to marry her. Since she would not take no for an answer, Ram's brother Lakshman cut her nose forcibly.

She complained to her brother Ravana who abducted Ram's wife Sita and brought her to Lanka, intent on making her his queen, despite her protests. Ram eventually attacked Lanka, killed Ravana and liberated Sita.

In her next life, Surpanakha desired to be Lakshman's wife. The gods agreed, but he would never be her husband. 'In that case, let

him be killed by Ravana reborn,' she said. And so, Surpanakha was reborn as Phulvati, Lakshman as Pabuji, and Ravana as Jindhrav Khinchi.

Phulvati learnt that Pabuji had managed to secure camels from faraway Lanka. So, she was determined to marry Pabuji. He agreed reluctantly, but after they had taken three of seven rounds around the sacred fire, he received words that Deval's cows had been stolen by Jindhrav Khinchi who had eyed them for long.

Deval was an old woman who had given Pabuji his magical horse, Kamal, and extracted the promise that he would always protect her cows. Pabuji had to keep this promise and so rushed to fight Jindhrav Khinchi. He died saving the cattle. Phulvati, his half-wife, committed Sati in his memory.

- The ballad of Pabuji is sung even today in Rajasthan amongst the community of camel herders. It is said he brought camels to Rajasthan in the tenth century.
- The idea of characters from Ramayana being reborn as folk heroes and heroines is a recurrent theme in Indian lore.
- The idea of a wedding getting interrupted by war is a recurring theme in folk ballads. It is found even in Indo-Islamic lore such as that of Ghazi Mian Pir and Johara Bibi where the hero leaves the wedding to save cattle from thieves and is killed. The wedding drum becomes the battle drum. Henna becomes blood. Ornaments and flowers become armour, and love songs are replaced by wailing.
- In Jain literature, Nemi-nath refuses to get married after

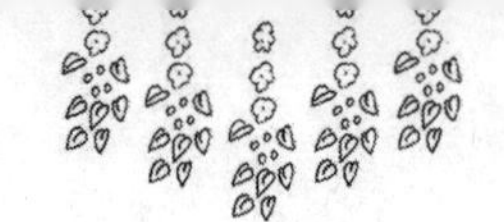

hearing the cries of animals about to be slaughtered for the wedding feast. Thus, marriage is linked to violence which is linked to sensual indulgence.

85. Urvashi Curses Arjuna

The beautiful Urvashi saw Arjuna in the celestial paradise known as Swarga and wanted to marry him.

But he rejected her advances. 'You were once married to my ancestor Pururava and you are much loved by my father, Indra. How can I marry you?'

Urvashi argued that she was immortal and a free woman. Rules of mortals and bound women did not apply to her.

'But they apply to me,' said Arjuna rejecting her proposal.

Urvashi became so angry that she cursed Arjuna to lose his male genitals and be a woman.

- The story comes from the Mahabharata.
- There are many tales of a celestial being wooing a mortal. Gods woo women. Goddesses woo men. Some unite, some do not. Pururava goes mad when Urvashi leaves him in boredom. Arjuna, wiser by that experience, prefers not to unite with Urvashi.
- In Telugu folklore, the goddess Gangamma approaches the hero Katamaraju but he rejects her advances saying that she is a goddess who he worships and so will not marry her. She persists, scattering his cows, and blocking their

movement, till he agrees to marry her. But he constantly finds excuses to not consummate the relationship. Thus, the goddess remains unsatisfied and there is tension between her and the hero. He is eventually killed in battle.

- In Tamil folklore, Kattavarayan falls in love with a brahmin's daughter after smelling the fragrance of the water she bathed in. He turns into a fish and gets entangled in her hair. When she sees him, she falls in love with him too. But they cannot unite as he is from the lowest caste, despite his beauty and valour. He is impaled at a stake and the love remains unrequitted.

86. Bahuchra's Betrayal

Once, a prince did not want to marry. But his parents forced him to tie the knot with a beautiful princess. Every night, the princess waited for her groom, but he would not come to her bed. Instead, he would ride into the forest on his horse.

The princess decided to investigate and followed the prince. As she had no horse, she rode a rooster and came upon a clearing in the forest where she found her husband having sex with other men.

'Why then did you marry me and ruin my life if you do not desire women?' she asked angrily. She then cut off his genitals and transformed into the goddess Bahuchra. The prince wore women's clothes and worshipped her, praying for his salvation.

- This story comes from the oral tradition of Gujarat and narrated by the hijras linked to the Bahuchra mata shrine.
- It draws attention to the plight of women forced to marry gay men. The wife is blamed for being unable to arouse desire in her husband.
- Unhappy wives turning into goddesses is a recurring theme in Indian folklore.

87. Punyakshi Becomes Kanyakumari

Punyakshi wanted to marry. The gods did not want that because she had the power to kill demons only as a virgin. To thwart her marriage plans, they declared that only a man who could give Punyakshi's father a betel leaf without veins, a sugarcane without rings and a coconut without eyes could claim her as his wife.

In answer to Punyakshi's prayer, Shiva conjured these gifts and became the chosen groom.

Punyakshi's father began wedding preparations and sent for the astrologer to decide an auspicious hour for the marriage ceremony. 'She can marry this very night or at the end of time,' said the astrologer who was in fact Indra in disguise. Shiva immediately set out from his mountainous abode in the north of India. Punyakshi's village stood at the southern tip of the continent. The journey was a long one and the gods were confident Shiva would not make it.

But Shiva used his powers and got his bull, Nandi, to fly. Fearing he would make it to the wedding, Indra took the form of a rooster and began to crow in the middle of the night. Tricked into thinking that it was daybreak and the auspicious hour of marriage had passed, Shiva turned around.

When dawn came and there was no sign of the groom, the wedding guests departed. Frustrated, Punyakshi kicked the pots of food prepared for the wedding banquet. These turned into grains of sand. She washed her face in the sea and the cosmetics coloured the sea. Demons mocked her fate and proposed marriage. In her rage, Punyakshi picked up her sickle and killed them all to the delight of the devas.

Punyakshi then stood on the southern tip of India and decided to wait for Shiva until the end of time. She became renowned as Kanyakumari, the virgin-goddess.

- Kanyakumari stands at the southern tip of India and this story explains the colours of the sand there. Her power prevents the sea from overwhelming the land.

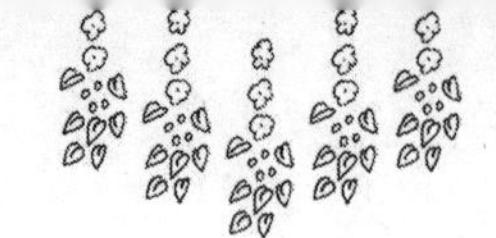

- The idea of marriage to contain the power of female deities is a recurring theme in Hindu lore. Energy is released through romantic and reproductive activity. The single goddess and the single god are seen as 'hot' and fiery.

88. Ayaman

In his former life, he was probably a bear or a monkey when Ram rescued Sita from Lanka. Out of respect he never looked at Sita's face, but he saw her feet and wondered how beautiful she would be if her feet were so delicate. The gods decided that he would be born as Ayaman, and marry Radha, but he would never be able to consummate his relationship with her.

So, Radha was married to Ayaman, but they never consummated their relationship. She loved Krishna, a relationship that would remain incomplete as Krishna would eventually leave the village and go to the city. And Ayaman would travel and perhaps have wives and lovers in other cities, but he would always come back to his wife, Radha, who pined for another, but served him as a dutiful spouse.

- The story of Radha is not found in Bhagavata Purana. It comes from the Sanskrit work of Jayadeva known as Gita Govinda which is about 1000 years old. More details of the

relationship come from folk songs found in Mithila, Bengal and Odisha.

- Radha is always considered as married to another (parakiya) and not married to Krishna (svakiya). Power of the relationship comes from its clandestine nature.
- Around a thousand years ago, we find in India stories that deal with at one hand chaste ascetics and on the other the cunning adulteress. This shifts after the rise of bhakti.
- In Radha lore, the extramarital nature of the relationship is made sacred. It is an acknowledgement of a relationship not legitimized by custom or law.

89. Dayamava

A thief fell in love with Dayamava, the daughter of a priest. Posing as a priest, he married her and brought her to his mother's house. Dayamava served her husband with devotion and bore him many children.

One day, during dinner, her mother-in-law remarked that the food tasted like an animal's tongue. Dayamava recoiled in horror and realized her husband was not the priest he claimed to be. Priests are supposed to be vegetarians.

An angry Dayamava raised a sickle, killed her mother-in-law and her children and burnt the house. In fear, her husband ran out in the form of a male buffalo. Dayamava chased him, caught him by the horns, pinned him down with her foot and beheaded him. She became the goddess, to whom buffaloes are offered each year.

- This story comes from oral traditions of Andhra Pradesh, Tamil Nadu and Karnataka.
- The theme deals with the rage of a woman duped by her husband, a recurring theme in goddess folklore. Unlike Durga, who kills the buffalo-demon to rescue the gods, in folk tradition, the killing is more personal.
- Retellings and recordings of this story introduce the lens of caste, with the woman who becomes goddess projected as high caste, and the husband who tricks her as low caste. She is pure and he is impure. The violence is thus justified.
- This story justifies participation of vegetarian communities in the village ritual of buffalo sacrifice. The killing is seen as punishment. But there are other stories where the sacrifice is a fertility ritual: the killing equated to making the land fecund with the seed/blood of the sacrifice.
- Male buffaloes were sacrificed in agricultural communities as they were not as useful as male cows (bulls) who could be castrated and used as beasts of burden.
- Offering the male to the goddess took away the guilt of killing an animal whose meat was relished as food.

90. Prajakta

There was once a plant who fell in love with the sun god, Surya. She adored him greatly, but he showed no interest in her. Heartbroken, she decided she would bloom only at night so that the sun would never experience her fragrance.

- This story is a folktale. It is contrasted with the tale of the lotus and sunflower that bloom whenever the sun is in the sky.
- Plants that are fragrant at night are feared as the haunt of ghosts and serpents.
- Marriages that take place at night follow Asura-muhurat as against marriages that take place during the day which is called Deva-muhurat.
- Some argue that weddings at night took place to avoid attention of invaders and thieves. That way the wedding party could travel during the day and arrive at dusk, and after rituals leave at dawn.
- Some argue that weddings take place at night so that the married couple can see the sacred stars linked to fidelity (Alkor or Arundhati next to Big Dipper or Sapta Rishi) and stability (Pole Star or Dhruv). Also, the moon is seen as more romantic than the sun, who is consumed by his own radiance.
- It is common practice amongst Hindus to refer to the wife's name before the husband as she is 'shri' the embodiment

of auspiciousness and prosperity, the diminutive double of Lakshmi in the household. So it is always Gauri-Shankar and Lakshmi-Narayana.

91. Tambaku

Tambaku was so ugly that no man wanted to marry her. Her father offered all his wealth to the man who agreed to accept Tambaku as bride. However, even the lure of wealth did not win Tambaku a husband.

She died of loneliness. The gods who had given her an ugly face felt responsible for her unhappiness. To make amends, they declared that in her next birth all men would desire her. Tambaku was therefore reborn as the tobacco plant whose leaves never leave the mouths of virile men.

- Tambaku story comes from the tribes of Central India.
- Portuguese introduced tobacco in India five centuries ago.
- In another tribal myth, Parvati secured the plant to control the appetite of her husband Shiva.

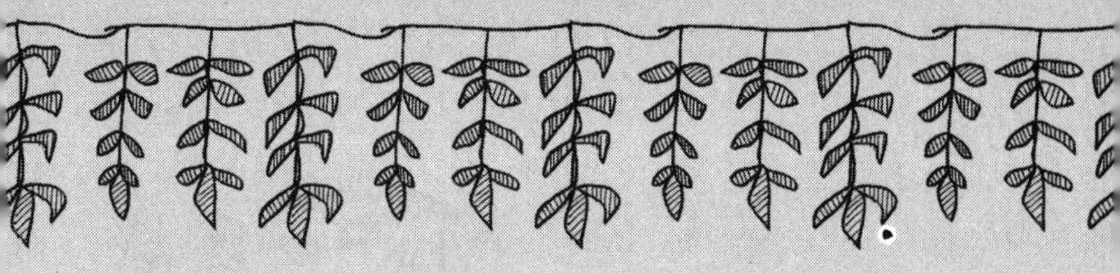

X

Coupledom

The divine always appears as a pair so much so that Vedic Sanskrit has a dual pronoun between the singular and the plural. In Vedic yagnas, gods came with male companions (Mitra-Varuna, Agni-Soma). In folk shrines, the goddess is joined by a female companion (Chamunda-Chotila, Nanda-Sunanda). In chaityas and mandirs, there is always at least one man and woman holding each other tenderly (Uma-Maheshwar, Lakshmi-Narayana). The pair embodies co-creation and inter-dependence, mutuality and reciprocity.

92. Gauri-Shankar

Bhringi expressed his desire to go around Shiva to express his devotion. As he was going around, Shiva's consort, Shakti, said, 'You cannot just go around him. You have to go around me too. We are two halves of the same truth.'

Bhringi, however, was so focused on Shiva that he had no desire to go around Shakti. Seeing this, Shakti sat on Shiva's lap making it difficult for Bhringi to go around Shiva alone. Bhringi then took the form of a snake and tried to slip in between the two. Amused by Bhringi's stubborn conduct, Shiva made Shakti one half of his body—the famous Ardhanareshwar form of Shiva. But Bhringi was adamant. He took the form of a bee and tried to bore his way between the two.

This annoyed the goddess so much that she said that Bhringi would lose all parts of the body that come from the mother. Instantly, Bhringi lost all flesh and blood and he became a bag of bones. He collapsed on the floor, unable to get up. Bhringi realized his folly. Shiva and Shakti are not independent entities. One cannot exist without the other.

- Bhringi's story is part of temple lore. In images, he is visualized as a skeleton standing erect on a tripod to remind everyone of the contribution of mothers. This is not scientifically true but a common tantric belief.

- In Bengali Krittibasa Ramayana, composed 500 years ago, widows of a king make love to each other after one of them drinks a magic potion and thus they are able to conceive a child named Bhagirāthi. Unfortunately, as no man is involved, the child is born without bones, reflecting tantric understanding of human reproduction.

- Jain tantra differentiated between the physical body (dravya-sharira) from the emotional body (sthula-sharira). Hindu tantra recognized a third body (karana-sharira), a social construct, based on estate and titles, that we create ourselves or comes to us because of fate. The physical body can be male (ida) and female (pingala). The psychological body is attracted to masculine (ida) and feminine (pingala) traits. The social body was made of clothes we wore and behaviour we exhibited. Tantra recognized that not all beings with male bodies, and male costumes, were attracted to feminine traits. Over 1500 years ago, these monk-scholars felt the need for the category 'queer', distinguishing the physical, from the biological and the social. These combinations and contradictions had to be resolved in society, and not through monastic practices. Monasticism was about knowing and accepting, not denying.

- Though Shiva accepts Shakti as one half of his body, there

are many tales of quarrels and separations, with Shiva taking refuge on Mount Kailash and Shakti going into the Deodar forest, until they reconcile. The separation and union of Shiva and Shakti reflects the rhythms of nature when forces split and bind again and again.

93. Saranya-Surya

Surya, the sun god, who rides a chariot pulled by seven horses, married Saranya, daughter of Tvastr-Vishwakarma, the divine craftsman. She gave him two sons and a daughter: Manu, Yama and Yami. But then one day she ran away, leaving behind her double, Chaya, who also gave Surya two sons and a daughter: another Manu, Shani and Tapati.

Surya did not notice the difference between Saranya and Chaya until one day he saw the mother curse Yama. How could a mother curse her own son, he wondered? He demanded an explanation and Chaya revealed she was just a double. The true wife had gone back to her father's house.

Surya went to Tvastr-Vishwakarma and sought an explanation. 'You are too full of yourself. Your power is too much for her to bear. And you did not even notice her absence. You are not a worthy husband,' said the father.

Surya begged his father-in-law to make him worthy of her. 'Tear out my power and turn it into weapons for the gods. Stripped of excess power, I will be worthy of my wife.' Tvastr-Vishwakarma removed a portion of the sun god's power and made weapons for the devas.

His power reduced; Surya went in search of his wife. He found her roaming in the form of a mare. He became a horse. Together they produced three sons: the Ashwin twins, who ride together on a chariot, and Revanta, the horse-rider.

- This story has been told repeatedly right from the Rig Veda, through the Brahmana literature, to the Puranas. It speaks of a husband transforming on realizing his flaws: his ignoring the wife, not noticing her absence, and eventually realizing the fault is with his dazzle (metaphor for ego).

- Does Surya, full of himself, not take no for an answer and force himself on his wife? Is that why Saranya leaves her husband? These are speculations that we can raise.

- Saranya's son and daughter, Yama and Yami, are linked to the tale of primal incest found in Rig Veda. As first man and woman, they have to make love to each other so that the human race can survive. Yama refuses and so becomes the first man to die, the king of the dead, who will never be reborn as he has left no children behind. Yami mourns his death by taking the form of night (Yamini) and the mournful river, Yamuna.

- Chaya's daughter, Tapati, is linked to arranged marriage in the Mahabharata. King Samavarna, while hunting in the forest, met her and proposed marriage. She asked him to send a priest to talk to her father. So Samavarna sent Rishi Vasishtha, and the wedding was fixed.

- The Ashwin twins are associated with marriage. They try

in vain to seduce the chaste Sukanya, wife of Chyavana. And they woo Suriya so she agrees to marry, either them or someone else.

- Revanta is considered the god of chase. A handsome and virile god, when he rides, women swoon. He was part of the solar cult that got absorbed into many folk cults, where hero-gods are shown riding white stallions, brandishing a stone. Many of these horse-riding hero-gods are called to battle on their wedding day, indicating the close link between sex and violence, marriage and property.
- Like Revanta, grooms are expected to ride to the bride's house on a mare, holding a sword. The mare-goddess is in folk tales of Raja Rasul, Pabuji; and Golu-dev, is the guardian-goddess of the rider.

94. Meenakshi-Somasundara

Meenakshi, princess of Madurai, was born with three breasts and a very masculine temperament. As soon as she ascended the throne after her father's death, she set out with her armies to conquer the world.

All the kings who opposed her ambitions were either defeated or killed. Finally, she reached Mount Kailas. The resident ascetic there insisted he was sovereign and would bow to no one.

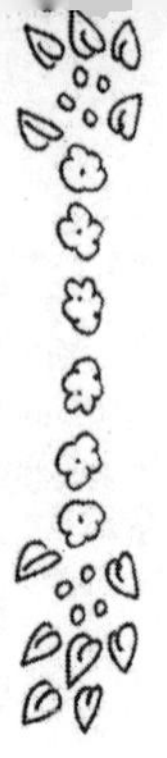

Furious, she challenged him to a duel.

As soon as she cast her eyes on the ascetic, however, she fell in love. Instantly her extra breast disappeared, and she became a demure maiden who invited the ascetic to her city and be her consort. The ascetic, who was Shiva, agreed. As Meenakshi's husband, he became known as Somasundara.

- Meenakshi's story is the temple lore of Madurai. South India is full of stories of lands ruled by women. But ruling is seen as a masculine trait and submitting a feminine trait. Here, the story is complex, as Meenakshi continues to rule and though she submits, the ascetic comes and stays in her house.

- Many communities in India transmitted property through women. Husbands would visit wives, but the property would belong to the wife and her children.

- Marriage transforms both men and women. Meenakshi becomes feminine, and demure, and the hermit Shiva becomes the householder Somasundara.

- In Tamil Nadu, people often ask if a household is like Chidambaram (where the husband dominates) or like Madurai (where the wife dominates).

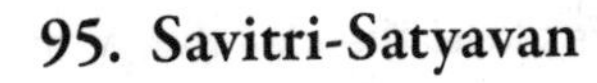

95. Savitri-Satyavan

Savitri, daughter of the king Ashvapati, was so beautiful and intelligent that men shied away from asking her hand in marriage. Ashvapati then told his daughter to travel to every kingdom in the land and look for a suitable groom.

As Savitri rode through the forest, she met a woodcutter called Satyavan and decided to marry him. Ashvapati was not pleased. Not only was Satyavan poor, but oracles predicted that he would die within a year of marriage. When Ashvapati saw that his daughter was determined to marry the man of her choice, he gave his consent and made arrangements for the wedding.

A year later, Yama, the god of death, arrived and claimed Satyavan's life. Instead of clinging to his corpse, Savitri followed Yama, determined to be with Satyavan even in the land of the dead. To stop her, Yama offered her a boon, anything but the life of her husband.

'Let Satyavan be the father of my children,' she said. Yama agreed but then for his boon to be true Satyavan would have to be alive and so the god of death was compelled to restore Satyavan back to life. Savitri became renowned as the woman who brought her husband back to life with her love and determination.

- Savitri's story comes from the Mahabharata. It is narrated to the Pandavas during their exile to show them the

power of a wife's love. The idea that a man's life is linked to a woman's love is a major theme in Hindu lore. Death is defeated by love.

- The story draws attention to men's discomfort with intelligent and rich women, and to respecting a woman's choice. It challenges the popular notion that all traditions oppressed women.

96. Priyamvada-Ruru

Ruru's beautiful wife, Priyamvada, died at an early age. Distraught, Ruru performed penance and invoked Yama, the god of death, and begged Yama to resurrect his wife.

After Ruru's great persistence, Yama decided to negotiate. Yama conveyed that if Ruru would give him half his life, he would give that half to Priyamvada. Thus, they could live together for a few more years.

Ruru agreed to give half his life to his wife. Priyamvada was restored back to life and both returned to the land of the living and lived many years together until it was time for both to die.

- This story comes from the Mahabharata. Stories often focus on how women's love save men's lives. But these are complementary stories, not often told, how men's love save women's lives.
- The love of a spouse does impact the quality of life, and maybe lifespan, of the partner. Unloved, we experience loneliness, anxiety and depression.
- The Ramayana tells the story of Aja, who could not bear to live after his young wife, Indumati, died prematurely. Likewise, we are told stories of women who die when they hear of their husband's death. This gives rise to the belief that husbands and wives who are truly in love are together in life and death over seven lifetimes.

97. Sita-Ram

Sita had been ever faithful to Ram. But life had treated her unfairly. She had followed Ram to the forest, when he was exiled by his father. She had stood by him in hardship. When Ravana kidnapped her, and tried to entice her with gifts and threats, she had stayed true to Ram. Yet, when Ram finally rescued her, he told her that she was free to marry the man she chose as he could not accept her as wife. For her reputation had been stained irrevocably, he could never install her as the queen of his kingdom.

Sita insisted on returning to Ayodhya with Ram. She walked through fire to prove her chastity. Still people on the streets

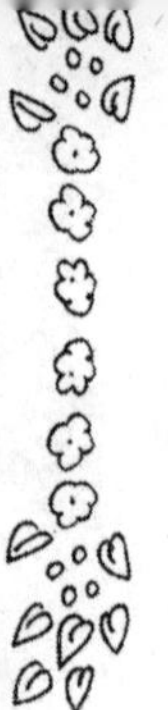

gossiped about her stay in Ravana's Lanka. Palace women asked her about Ravana and told her to draw his shadow on the wall of the palace. Her innocent actions spawned more gossip and suspicion.

Finally, Ram decided he had to abandon her. She was sent to the forest. Nobody cared that she was pregnant. Alone, in the wild, she gave birth to her two sons, Luv and Kush, and raised them alone. She never said anything negative about her husband. She even got the children to sing Valmiki's Ramayana, which glorified Ram's many adventures.

Ram never remarried. He replaced Sita with a statue, made of gold, declaring her purity. He never doubted her fidelity. He had rejected the queen of stained reputation, never the wife.

Years later, Ram came to the forest to fetch his sons, heirs to his throne. He did not ask Sita to return to Ayodhya. Sita told Ram to take care of her sons and heartbroken by the rejection, caused the earth to swallow her.

Sita found a home in Nag-lok, the land of serpents. She missed her children. So, the serpent-king Vasuki got his serpents to abduct Luv and Kush, and bring them to Nag-lok. Hanuman then came to rescue Ram's sons, and in the fight that followed, Hanuman found himself entangled by snakes.

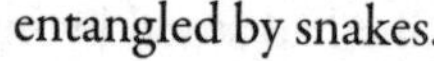

Finally, it was agreed that the children would live half the year above ground with Ram and half the year below ground with Sita. Sometimes Luv would stay with Ram all year round and Kush would stay with

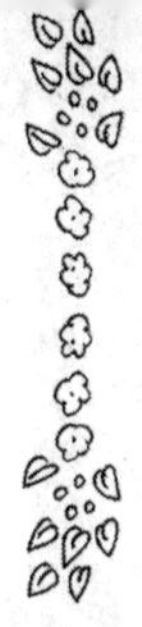

Sita. Then Kush would stay with Ram and Luv with Sita. Thus, the two children lived, divided between both parents.

When the twins were old enough to rule his kingdom, Ram decided he had no desire to live on earth without Sita. So, he entered the river Sarayu and never rose again.

- The story of Sita and Ram has hundreds of retellings with many twists and turns. There is no standard version, though Valmiki's Sanskrit retelling remains the oldest. This too has many manuscripts, with many variations between them. The story of Sita in Nag-lok asking the snakes to bring her children comes from the Assamese Adbhut Ramayana. It reveals the plight of children in families where husband and wife live separately.
- The Ramayana is the story of a king, not a husband. It draws upon the tension between public roles and private relationships. Private trust is often ignored in public matters, where reputation matters. A king's marriage is a public spectacle, not a private matter.

98. Urmila-Lakshman

Lakshman's wife, Urmila, wanted to follow her husband to the forest as Sita had followed Ram but Lakshman begged her to stay back. He asked her to take care of the family, as he would be too busy taking care of Sita and Ram. Urmila stayed back reluctantly wondering how she could help her husband help Ram.

On the first night in the forest, Lakshman kept watch while Ram and Sita went to sleep. That is when Nidra, the goddess of sleep, approached him. He begged the goddess to leave him alone for fourteen years so that he could guard his brother and sister-in-law night and day. The goddess, impressed by his act of filial devotion, agreed.

But the law of nature demanded that someone bear the burden of Lakshman's share of sleep. Ask Urmila, said Lakshman. Urmila agreed to sleep on Lakshman's behalf. So, it came to pass that Urmila slept for fourteen years night and day while her husband stayed awake in the service of Ram and Sita.

Because Lakshman had stayed awake for fourteen years, he was able to kill Ravana's mighty son, Meghnad, who could only be killed by a man who had not slept for at least twelve years.

- Urmila's story is part of many folk Ramayanas retold in regional languages including Telugu, Bengali, Odia and Marathi.

- The Ramayana deals with the complexities of conjugal relationships through stories such as these. Mandodari has to deal with a husband who yearns for other men's wives. Surpanakha has to deal with sexual desire after the death of her husband. Dasharatha has to deal with the complexities emerging from having three wives. Rishi Gautama has to deal with adultery and cuckoldry. Rishi Vasishtha and Rishi

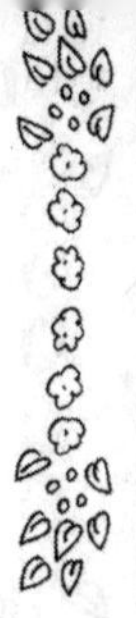

Atri have wives who are chaste. Sugriva remarries Vali's widow. Hanuman chooses celibacy. Vedavati yearns to marry Ram but her wish is unfulfilled.

99. Indrajit-Sulochana

Ram attacked the island-kingdom of Lanka with his army of monkeys to rescue his wife, Sita, abducted by the rakshasa-king Ravana, and locked in his garden. Ravan's son, Indrajit, also known as Meghnad, defended his father's citadel. But in the fight, he lost his life. His soldiers ran back into the citadel leaving his body on the battleground. Ravana feared his son's body would be abused by the monkeys but dared not step out to fetch it.

Lakshman's arrow that had severed Indrajit's head had carried the head into Ravana's citadel. Holding this head, Indrajit's wife Sulochana, came into the battlefield and requested Ram to give her the rest of her husband's body so that she could cremate him and join him in his journey to the land of the dead.

Ram was impressed by the fearlessness and fidelity of Sulochana and told his monkeys to handover Indrajit's body to the lady and help her take it back to Ravana's citadel.

- This story comes from folk traditions where Sulochana is considered a Naga princess and she performs 'sati'.
- The story was popularized when Michael Madhusudan

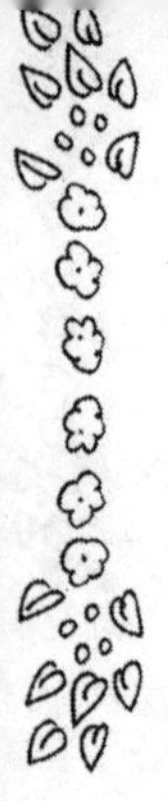

Dutt composed 'Meghnad Vadh' which saw the Ramayana as a Greek tragedy. Indrajit or Meghnad, known as Beerbahu in the retelling, is equated with Hector and Ravana with King Priam of Troy, and Sita with Helen, even though Sita is abducted by Ravana and Helen eloped with Paris, the prince of Troy. Beerbahu's wife who performs sati is called Prameela.

- In the Ramayana, many of Ravana's wives become satis. In the Mahabharata, many of Krishna's wives become satis. Scholars believe that since sati was not prevalent in Vedic times, these epics, after centuries of oral transmission, were written in times when the sati practice was prevalent or at least venerated.

100. Damyanti-Nala

Rejecting even the proposals of the gods, Damyanti chose to marry Nala. They lived a happy life for many years until one day Nala gambled away his fortune and the couple was reduced to poverty, with nothing but the clothes on their bodies.

Nala asked Damyanti to go back to her father's house but she refused to leave his side. Nala felt like a loser, and ran away at night, while she slept, hoping she would forget about him, maybe even remarry. He made himself ugly so no one recognized him and worked as a cook in a faraway land, so ashamed he was of what he had done.

Damyanti refused to give up on Nala. She survived the forest, wild animals, rapists, thieves, and kept searching for Nala. She tracked him down because travelling bards told her of King Rituparna's cook who made the best food in the world and who could also solve puzzles and compose songs. Such a talented man, even if he was a servant, had to be her Nala.

Damyanti sent word to Nala that she still loved him and was patiently waiting for his return, whenever he was ready. Motivated by Damyanti's resilience, Nala learnt the tricks of gambling, recovered his fortune from those who had stolen it, apologized to Damayanti and took her back to the house that was once their home. They lived happily together, forever.

- The story comes from the Mahabharata and is the story of resilience through the vagaries of life. Damyanti stands by Nala, even when he is broken, and has lost everything. She enables him to recover.
- The scriptures put the burden of support on the women, not the man. We can read this literally or metaphorically. Literally, we stereotype men and women. Metaphorically, we recognize that drive to succeed needs to be balanced by the drive to accept failures. Both these drives can be wrapped in male or female bodies, and in a relationship both drives are needed.

- The Mahabharata stories continuously refer to the possibility of Damyanti remarrying, indicating that in epic times, remarriage was not a taboo and one could remarry if the husband went missing or was incompetent, or did not keep the wife happy.

Conclusion: Different Heavens Make Different Marriages

सखा सप्तपदा भव।
सखायौ सप्तपदा बभूव।
सख्यं ते गमेयम्।
सख्यात् ते मायोषम्।
सख्यान्मे मयोष्ठाः।

You have walked seven steps with me; be my friend.
We have walked seven steps together; let us be friends.
Let me get your friendship.
Let me not part from your friendship.
May you not part from my friendship.

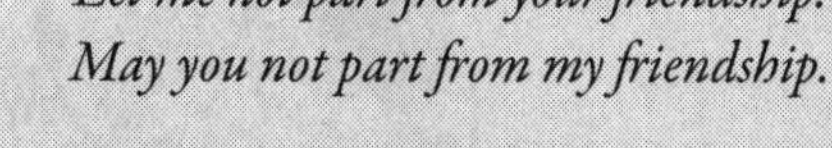

In India, there are wedding ceremonies at day and wedding ceremonies at night, weddings that involve going around a fire, and weddings that involve tying a thread, weddings that focus on paperwork and weddings where it is all about rituals. Weddings in temples take place in seconds, weddings at homes may go on for days. Sometimes the groom comes to fetch the bride, at other times, the bride and the groom meet at a banquet hall. Some grooms come riding mares, some cover their face with veils, some brides leave with a smile, others with a tear. Some weddings involve dowry, others involve charity. Some weddings are silent and solemn, others full of song, dance and drunken revelry.

While everyone sees the diversity of wedding rituals, we rarely see the diversity of wedding beliefs.

In Shiva temples, the divine couple clings to each other. In Vishnu temples, the goddess has her own separate shrine. Ram is faithful to a single wife; Krishna adores many wives, but in temples stands alone, or with Radha, who is not his wife, at least not in the mundane earthly sense. Goddesses in temples dress as brides but there is no husband in sight. They are called the virgin (kumari) but also mothers (mata). No one is sure if that means she is untouched by a man, or unattached to any single man, pure or sovereign.

For centuries, India had ascetics and courtesans who never

married but played a key role in shaping Indian culture. Just because you did not have sex, or had sex with many people, does not mean you did not have companions and partners who loved you and who cared for you, children you cared for and who cared for you, property you inherited and bequeathed, families of choice, unbound by blood and law. This was acknowledged in sacred stories—in the love of Radha for Krishna, in the bond between Matsyendranath and Gorakhnath, and in the collective families of the Kritikas, Matrikas and Yoginis.

In trying to convert Hinduism to a religion under colonial pressure, there has been a desperate rush for homogenizing and standardizing the diverse Hindu rituals and beliefs. People are guided by the hegemonic monotheistic principle: there can be no false gods, only one true god. And so the wedding certificate provided by the state effectively became the true god, negating the power of the sacred ritual that once impacted the heart and mind. Wedding rituals have today been reduced to a fun-filled stage performance for the faithful.

The state simply assumes heterosexuality, monogamy and patriarchy is the norm, like colonial masters of yore. The British who used the dharma-shastra to make Indian laws ignored the fact that the dharma-shastra was meant primarily for brahmin and the land-owning elite. They were never for all communities. The rishis always valued local practices: different gods for different folks.

We are often told that divorce was not Indian; but there were many Indian communities where divorce was common. So when the Indian state adopted it, they were not importing any alien value. We are told that widow remarriage is not common; but they were common in many communities. There were communities where only one daughter-in-law is allowed into the household to prevent breakup of property, communities where property is passed on not to the eldest son but the youngest daughter, or to the child who took care of the old parents. There are communities where sex is not a necessary part of marriage, and where marrying a plant, an animal, a rock or a god, is not weird.

We often confuse diversity with hierarchy and so create divisions like high/low, refined/raw, urban/rural/tribal, classical/folk, civilized/crude. In doing so, we privilege practices at the centre of power and wealth, not at the edge of forests. We see the centre as sacred and pure, and the periphery as profane and polluted. Rishis never did this: they saw everything is suitable for its context. Hence, they aggregated truths.

There are no false gods in Hinduism; no false rituals; no false beliefs. Just different beliefs for different needs and different temperaments. When you seek to homogenize such a diversity for the sake of political unity, you end up privileging a few communities and their practices over others. Usually that of the elite. When the strong dominate the weak, culture follows the matsya nyaya (fish justice) where strong eat weak. When the strong enable the weak, it is dharma. Dharma demands expansion (brah-) of the heart and mind (manas) to include the different and the many. That is why God in Hinduism is called brahman, who is infinite (anant).

Mimicking the ways of monotheism, Hindi is being privileged over tribal languages in the name of unity. But Hindi does not capture the totality of Hindustan, or Hinduism. No language does. Even Hindi is not monolithic: there are several Hindis, each with its own nuance, from Maithili to Awadhi to Braj-bhasha to Bhojpuri. Every language-god once thrived in India, before we were forced to classify and prioritize them, in the name of efficiency.

Likewise, people assume that all Hindus are vegetarians or that all Brahmins are vegetarians. Both statements are false. Census reveals most Indians are non-vegetarians. There are many modern politicians who want to claim 'tribal' communities as Hindu, in order to rescue Hinduism from missionaries, but they reject tribal ways. Brahmin communities from Odisha, Bengal, Mithila, Konkan and Kashmir eat fish and meat, even chicken. There is no standard diet. And creating hierarchies on food, defining what is 'correct Hindu food', simply reveals an inability to rise above caste hierarchies and religious prejudices, which is indicative of the insecure ego (aham) not the secure spirit (atma).

No single wedding belief or practice encompasses all of India, or humanity. The Rishi understood diversity as an expression of the divine. He/she would not expect the swan to marry like a snake or the snake to marry like a swan. The rishi would not privilege one over the other, either. The snake can be a swan in its next life, and the swan can be a snake in its next life. But for that to happen, they have to first reproduce in their own way.

Humans are neither swans nor snakes. We have the imagination to break all boundaries, reimagine all categories, and accommodate much more, as we expand (brah-) our hearts and minds (manas) and make the expansive spiritual journey towards the infinite (ananta) divine (brahman).

- In a traditional Vedic wedding, the groom and the bride are temporary deities, earthly manifestations of god and goddess which is why they are adorned with gold, turmeric, sandal paste, flowers and crowns. They are not expected to bow to elders until the ritual is over.

- The marriage ritual is meant to bring about a shift in consciousness as a rite of passage, hence the importance of fasting and staying awake at night, and the unending rituals involving gods, ancestors, parents and family.

- Feeding guests at the wedding was the only way to get witnesses in days before the 'marriage certificate' became key to establish legitimacy of marriage.

- In ancient India, God was never a witness to the marriage as in Judeo-Christian-Islamic weddings. Gods and ancestors came as guests and were entertained with song and dance and food, like human guests.

- The wedding in India was a caste and community affair. The state did not play any role except in resolving inter-caste disputes. Hindus did not have the concept of registering a marriage as in Judaism, Christianity and Islam. It came into being as the culture of documentation emerged in British Raj and later rise of Indian nation-state.

- The British confused dharma-shastras, which were meant only for brahmins and the land-owning elite, as codes for all of Indian society. And so, many people think wedding rituals described in Sanskrit texts are 'correct' Hindu rituals. They are not. Even the presence of Brahmin in a wedding is not required in most communities, though this is being 'standardized'. Vedic 'sapta padi' is for all forms of agreement; not just marriage. The 'sindoor' of eastern India is not seen in south India, and the 'thali' of south India is not seen in north India, and the 'ghodi' of baraats in north India are not seen in the rest of India.

- As the world becomes increasingly gender-neutral, as women are being seen as individuals not baby-making machines, there are calls for allowing same-sex marriages.
- Today the spiritual aspects of the wedding are overshadowed by the social and legal aspects of the wedding. The marriage is seen as an economic and political affair that grants the spouse property rights, as well as rights related to taking decisions on health matters.

Appendix 1: How to Conduct a Modern Indian Wedding

When people refer to an Indian wedding, they are referring to the pomp and ceremony mostly seen in elite Hindu weddings; weddings that happen among the members of the upper caste and the upper class, with the wherewithal to fund such lavish affairs. What is unique about Hindu weddings is that it is not viewed as a contract, as in an Islamic wedding. There is no promise made; no contract signed. It is rather performative, full of symbolic rituals with deep metaphors, related to union and fortune. Also, the brahmin is not legitimizing or solemnizing the wedding as the Jewish rabbi, or the Catholic or Zoroastrian priest. The brahmin is simply enabling the rite of passage by chanting Vedic hymns that traditionally only he can chant—this is changing now. In many communities, no Vedic hymns are required, and women conduct the wedding. In fact, the idea of a Vedic wedding was popularized by Arya Samaj only in the nineteenth century. Historically speaking, the inclusion of Vedic hymns and brahmins increased with a process called 'Sanskritization' whereby a community sought to identify itself as elite. It also increased when Persian

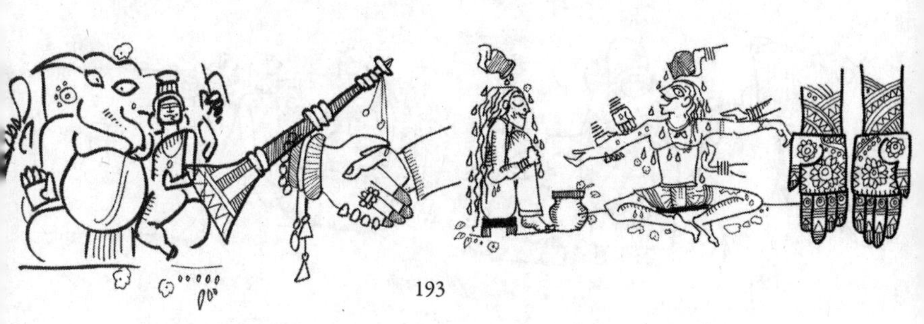

and colonial authorities assumed that Vedas and brahmins were indicative of the most refined Indian culture. Brahmin and 'upper caste' wedding rituals with hymns are based on Vedas and elaborated in the Grihasutras and Dharma-shastras.

God does not solemnize the Hindu wedding as in Christian, Sikh and Zoroastrian ceremonies. In Hindu weddings, the groom and the bride are themselves seen as gods (vara-vadhu-devata), emulating Shiva and Shakti, Vishnu and Lakshmi, at least temporarily, which is why the lavish clothing, including garlands and crowns. All gods (vishwadeva) and all ancestors (pitr) are invited to assemble, just like human guests: to witness the union, enjoy the food, the entertainment, and, in exchange, bless the couple. For everything in Hinduism is a voluntary exchange, a yagna!

At one time, Hindu women chose their husbands (swayam-vara). At one time, love marriage was celebrated (gandharva-vivah). But over time, it was believed that women had to be controlled by fathers, brothers, husbands and sons. They had to be sought (prajapati-vivah), or offered with dowry (brahma-vivah), given as payment (deva-vivah), or sold (asura-vivah). Daughters were seen as the wealth of an outsider (paraya-dhan), held in trusteeship by her father, until her wedding, in which she would be given away (kanyadaan) and her hand received (panigrahan) by the groom. Marriage was a partnership hence the seven-step ritual (sapta padi), but success depended on the wife seeing her husband as the only god who mattered (pati-parmeshwar).

In many communities, marriage was when her name, not just surname, and her lineage (gotra) was changed forever, officially.

Like all things Hindu, rituals and meaning of rituals are changing with time (kala) and place (sthan) and people (patra) involved. Today, gender equality plays an important role. Marriage is expected to be between equals, with mutual consent. Dowry is seen as illegal by the state though continues to be secretly indulged in, seen as tradition, or the only way to give the daughter a share of wealth because until recently she had no legal rights on parental property.

Indian weddings vary as per regions, caste, personal beliefs and economic status. Also, the wedding ritual has transformed over time. It is tough to replicate the wedding rituals of old, static agricultural communities in modern industrial urban societies. We live in times where global Indian culture is defined by Bollywood kitsch. So, we need wedding planners and wedding designers. Not to mention the media team.

Broadly the modern Indian wedding has ten parts:

1. Agreement
2. Preparations
3. Invitations
4. Arrival of the Groom
5. Union
6. Symbols
7. Games

8. Departure of the Bride
9. Entry of the Bride
10. Registration

1. Agreement

Most Indian weddings are family affairs. So, the man does not propose with a ring. In fact, until recently, the groom and the bride never saw each other's face until the wedding ceremony. The wedding agreement was done by parents in their absence, sometimes when they were not even born, or when they were children. The proposal is still followed by intense conversations with astrologers (who match horoscopes), priests (who check gotra) and accountants and lawyers (in case of dowry). Agreement is ceremonially marked by exchange of gifts, something for the bride and something for the groom. Usually, heirlooms are exchanged to mark the union of families.

Weddings are stressful times for both families. For the bride's family, it involves huge expenses that can ruin them, unless the groom agrees to share expenses. For the groom's family, the greatest fear is of the breakup of the family as daughters-in-law become a new power competing with the mother-in-law or with the other women of the household. One of the reasons why the Ramayana is valued more than the Mahabharata in India, is

because Sita in Ramayana does not divide the family as Draupadi in the Mahabharata does.

2. Preparations

On the day before the wedding, or on days leading up to the wedding, the bride and the groom are prepared. They are teased, warned and educated about the changes that will follow the wedding through wedding songs, accompanied by music and dance. There are functions conducted by friends and sisters for the bride, and functions conducted by the friends and brothers for the groom. This has become increasingly popular, thanks to Bollywood movies and television serials. The song and dance celebration known as 'sangeet' was more of a North Indian custom, but has now spread to the east and south, and beyond Indian shores, complete with professional choreographers.

Just before the wedding, the bride and the groom are bathed (mangala snan) with turmeric (haldi) to make their skin glow. This is done by the women of the house who also wave lamps to usher in positive energy and put kohl (kajal) around the girl's eyes to remove negative energy. Applying henna or mehndi (that came to India with the Persians, Turks and Arabs around twelfth century) on the hands and legs is now an integral part of the ceremony. In the east and south, instead of henna, people use alta or red dye. The

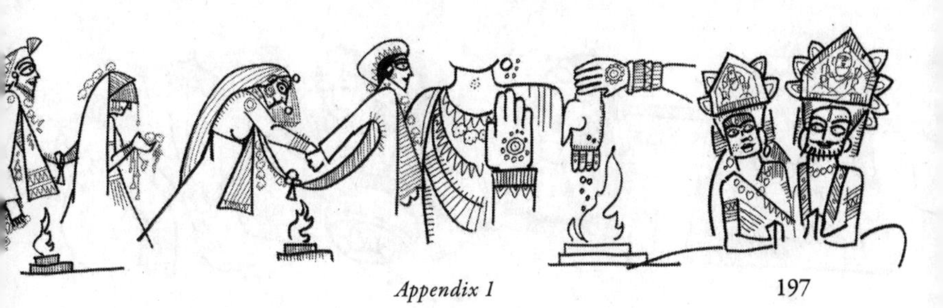

bride and groom are not just made beautiful, they are transformed into deities. The rituals were at one time led by women who were married and whose husbands were alive, so considered auspicious (sadhava, suhagan, sumangali). They functioned like priestesses, transmitters of good luck. In Assam, the groom's mother comes to the bride's house and helps her get ready, bringing water in a pot and giving her a coin (for prosperity) and knife (for protection). The bride eats half a cup of curd and the groom's mother takes the remaining cup back home to her son.

An important role used to be played by the barber (nai) who, of all the castes in the village, would be allowed to enter every household, and so often functioned as village matchmaker. His wife also used to be the hairdresser. There were at one time special castes that specialized in makeup and jewellery. Weddings involved weavers, potters, cooks—the entire village, especially, if it involved the headman.

Dressing up (shringar) to make the body worthy of marriage is a key ceremony in Hindu rituals, as it is in temples. Traditionally sixteen items adorn the bride, and that includes clothing, jewellery, flowers, fragrance and mouth fresheners. Lopamudra would not let her husband Agastya touch her until he had made himself worthy. Apala begs Indra to make her worthy of her husband. Everyone agrees that unhappy unions result in unhappy children.

3. Invitations

Everyone is invited to the wedding. It is important to take care of the guests, feed them and seek their blessings. Guests served as witnesses to a wedding, in the days before documentation and registration. Gods and goddesses are also invited to the wedding. So are the ancestors. The bride worships Gowri, or Parvati, the perfect wife. The groom worships Ganesha, the good son, remover of obstacles. Special ceremonies are held to invite ancestors. Traditionally, arrival of ancestors is considered inauspicious as death is regarded as pollution, and so special rooms or corners are identified where the ancestors can be entertained with food. They don't have to mingle with the other guests.

In the old days, before recording technology, singers and dancers were invited to entertain the family. This included the courtesans, the tawaifs, who were highly talented and skilled. These women were not expected to marry; they were seen as eternally married (sada-suhagan). Their presence brought good luck. Also included were transgender performers (hijras) who were called to remove the evil eye (nazar). They often participated in rituals to remove bad luck and usher in good luck.

In Vedic times, the proposal was sent to the bride's house as suggested in the Rig Vedic wedding hymn. After she accepted, the groom would set out. But nowadays, the invitation is sent from the bride's house, usually handed over by the bride's brother. In

case of child marriages, the invitation was sent to tell the groom that the bride had matured, and it was time for him to fetch her.

Everyone who comes is fed. The wedding feast is an integral part of the wedding. A well-fed guest is likely to give the best blessing to the couple. The banquet may be vegetarian or non-vegetarian, with or without alcohol. It varies between communities.

4. Arrival of the Groom

The groom travels with his family and friends to the bride's house. In North India, he travels on a mare and his face is covered with a veil made of flowers (sehra). These practices probably came with old horse-riding communities who entered India from the Northwest (Sakas, Kushan, Turk). In many local legends of North India especially, we find the guardian goddess taking form of the mare to protect heroes such as Tejaji, Pabuji and Ramdev-pir. The sehra also protected the handsome, bedecked groom from the evil eye, for he could very well attract the attention of sexual predators who haunted forests, highways and crossroads. The sword-holding reinforced the Rajput status and was temporarily given to other communities too as the groom was seen as a god during the period of ritual. In casteist societies, caste hierarchy is reinforced by not letting 'lower' caste men ride horses. They had to ride buffaloes instead.

Kings preferred travelling on elephants. In other parts of India, the groom came by foot. The procession is full of lights and music. Drums are beaten, horns are blown, lamps are lit. This is to scare away the ghosts and to tell the world that a special event is taking place—a turning in the lifecycle of a man. On the way to the bride's house, prayers are offered to family gods, and village gods, and other guardian gods. And while the groom is away, the women of his household have fun, singing songs full of 'bawdy' lyrics for it is the few times in the household and village when men are not around.

The groom is often accompanied by a young male relative. Called the 'little groom' , in the old days he would also be seen as responsible for bride if anything happened to the groom. In some communities a widow would be expected to marry the little groom or a younger brother in law.

When the groom arrives at the bride's house, he is received by the bride's family, especially the women. He is seen as a form of Shiva and Vishnu. His feet are washed, anointed with turmeric and sandal paste, lamps would be waived around his face, he would be sprinkled with perfume, offered sweets and flowers and gifts, and ushered in, along with his guests who are also welcomed with food, music and flowers. The arrival of the groom is an important theme in Shiva Purana, where Shiva comes dressed as a ferocious mendicant bedecked with ash and snakes, to the horror of Parvati's mother-in-law. This is the moment when the bride's

mother ensures the groom is worthy of her daughter.

5. Union

The main wedding ceremony is held under a pavilion (kalayan mandap), rendered auspicious with many fertility symbols such as pots, banana plants, coconuts, swastika and symbolic representations of couples and households.

The ceremony can be very short. In many South Indian communities, it simply involves the boy tying the sacred thread (mangal-sutra) around the bride's neck, to the sound of music, and in the presence of relatives. The mangal-sutra is made of beads and has a special medallion (thali) with different designs for different communities. In Telugu weddings, the knot is tied three times indicating union of thc three bodies: mind, body and property. In other parts of India, the ritual can go on for hours, either at day or at night, exhausting the bride and the groom, who are often expected to fast. This is how rituals of a rite of passage ensures shift in consciousness—the realization that their life is going to be different henceforth.

There are rituals involving only the groom and only the bride, before the two meet and sit together. The meeting is often dramatic with a curtain kept between the two, so that the parting of the curtain is celebrated to the sound of music and the shower

of rice and flowers. It is similar to the excitement that is seen in Hindu temples when the door of the inner sanctum is opened to reveal the elaborately bedecked deity enshrined inside. In some communities, the girl's face is shown to the groom for the first time reflected in a plate of water, or a mirror. Remember, the bride and the groom are seen as gods for that moment. So, this is the meeting of gods: Shiva and Shakti, Purusha and Prakriti. In Bengal, the bride is carried by her brothers and uncles, her face covered with a betel leaf. In Maharashtra, the priest shouts 'be alert' (savadhan)—warning and preparing the bride and groom for the momentous transformation that awaits them. In Odisha, both the groom and the bride wear crowns and their face is painted with sandal paste to enhance their eyes, like deities being worshipped.

The bride's father then gives the daughter's hand to the groom (kanyadaan) and he receives it (panigrahan), the groom's upper garment is tied to the bride's upper garment, the knot (gaanth bandhan) representing union. In Telugu weddings, the most important ceremony is when the bride and the groom mix a paste of cumin and jaggery between their palms. In North India, the most important ceremony is the exchange of garlands (jay mala).

Then, as newlyweds, the couple takes seven steps together that makes them partners (dampatya). They may walk around the fire seven times (saat-phera), sometimes led by the bride, sometimes the groom. In Vedic times, the seven steps ritual was

for all partnerships, not just for marriage. The seven steps are seven things the couple has to share; though now, influenced by Christian weddings, it is seen as seven vows. Jewish weddings also have seven blessings, and the bride goes around the groom seven times. In Sikh weddings, the couple goes around the holy book four times when four songs are sung to remind the couple, they are not two bodies sitting next to each other, but one soul united.

In the east, the groom puts red vermillion powder (sindoor) on the parting of the woman's head. There are rituals where the groom places his palm on his wife's heart seeking access to her love. There are rituals where he touches her big toe and places it on a rock, seeking her firm support in hard times. Finally, the bride and the groom make offerings to the gods for the first time as a couple (laja homa), assisted by the bride's brother, who visits his sister annually during Diwali, to ensure she is well taken care of. The bride is Lakshmi, goddess of fortune, being given to Vishnu, who will transform his house into Vaikuntha and the brother is Yama, god of accounting, keeping an eye on her welfare.

6. Symbols

Hindu rituals are full of symbols. If the Christian bride wears white to express virginity, the Hindu bride, like the Chinese bride, is bedecked in red and gold that expresses fertility. Around

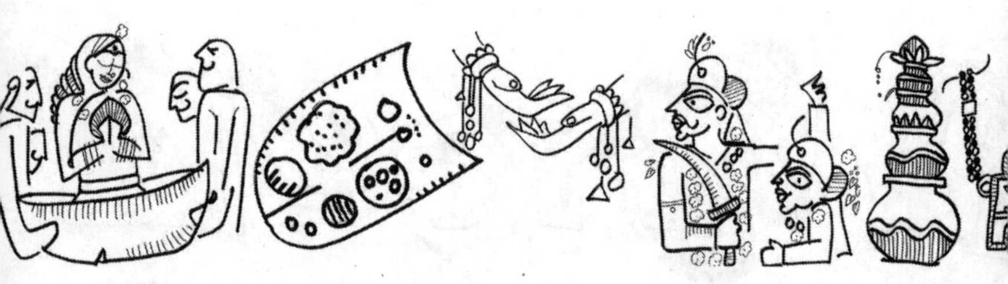

the wedding altar, symbols of fertility abound. There are plant symbols (coconut, banana, mango leaves, rice, betel nut, betel leaf, turmeric, dry fruits), animal symbols (parrots, butterflies, cows), human symbols (palm prints, foot prints, effigies of couples in a home, artifacts (pots, cloth, lamp, perfumes) as well as abstract symbols (crisscrossing triangles, swastika, three dots). The floor and walls of the wedding area are painted with traditional and modern art. In Mithila, Bihar, a corner of the bride's house (kobhar ghar) is painted with special fertility symbols such as lotuses, fish, parrots, elephants, mango, water. In some communities, this is the nuptial chamber where the couple spends their first night. The next day elder women check the bed if it has been stained red to confirm consummation. Only then does the couple depart to the groom's house.

Symbols extend from house to body. Monks are identified with shaven heads or matted hair, widows by wearing white or ochre and no ornaments. Everyone except widows and monks and nuns are expected to be married in India. Single women announce their single status by not wearing symbols of marriage, and so are also constantly questioned. Single men cannot be distinguished from married men, which proves awkward for men who choose to be single. Men are not expected to wear any symbol of marriage, though nowadays some choose to wear wedding bands as popularized by Hollywood films.

Symbols of marriage for women include nose-ring, toe-ring,

bangles, sindoor on the forehead as a dot (bindi) and smearing the parting of the hair, special chains around the neck. Punjabi brides are famous for the lac bangles (chuda); Bengali brides for their conch-shell bangles (shankha); Bihari brides for their sindoor; Marathi, Kannada, Tulu, Konkani, Malayali, Tamil and Telugu brides for their mangal-sutra, beaded and with special medallions. Kashmiri brides for their earrings passed through the ear-cartilage, a reminder of Kashmir Shaivism's close link with split-ear ascetics (Kanphata-nath-jogis).

7. Games

When Sita was alone in Lanka, she invented solitaire. Parvati invented ludo so that she could play with her husband and two sons. The idea of the couple playing games is a recurrent theme in Indian culture. The man and the woman sit on swings and enjoy spring and autumn. They go on boat rides. This is part of temple festivals too. And in weddings, the newlyweds are expected to play games to familiarize themselves with each other's touch. So, the bride is asked to open the groom's fist, in which he holds a gift for her. And they are asked to find a ring hidden in a pot of milk.

In Deccan regions, the bride and the groom shower each other with coloured rice, indicating the prosperity they bring to each other's life. They also press each other's toes ceremonially.

The couple is asked to feed each other. There are rituals where the groom and the bride are placed on a swing and asked to see the sun, the moon, the Pole Star and the Alkor (Arundhati) star, which are symbols of stability and love. Such games are played in the bride's house and in the groom's house.

Additionally, stories of happy married couples are told to the newlyweds as they embark on a new life.

8. Departure of the Bride

The departure of the bride (bidai) is a tearful event in most households. The reason for this cannot be appreciated in modern times where family is a video call away. In the old days, it was quite possible that the bride would never meet her family again, except during the annual visit by her brother, on Bhai dooj, if he lived nearby, or if she was allowed to visit him during Raksha bandhan, or maybe at a fair (mela) frequented by both families. The daughter-in-law, in traditional households, entered the husband's house as a bride and was expected to leave it as bride (either dying before her husband, or dying with her husband as sati). If she became a widow, she was sidelined, maybe even abandoned in a widow's home in Kashi or Mathura. This was the fate of women in elite households of North India. The bride's tearful farewell, popularized in North Indian songs, must be seen in this context.

In Kerala, in Nair families, the women never left the natal house; they were visited by husbands at night. They had the option to reject husbands and select new ones. In these communities, there were no farewell songs for the bride.

To delay the departure, the shoes of the groom would be stolen by sisters-in-law and be returned when he paid them money. Exchange of money and gifts at various points of the wedding was sometimes playful and sometimes a display of affluence. When the bride left the house in Bengal, she threw a fistful of rice behind her to repay her debts to her family; she owed them nothing thereafter. In North India, the woman left palm prints on the wall of her mother's house before leaving. And coconuts would be crushed under the wheel of the carts that took the bride away, crushing old relationships and demons who threatened the union and the return journey.

9. Entry of Bride

If the departure of a bride is a tragic episode, then the arrival of the bride in the groom's house is an exciting and auspicious event. Conch-shells are blown, drums are beaten, and women ululate (in Odisha and Bengal), crackers are burst (in Gujarat and Rajasthan). The woman enters kicking a pot of rice placed on the threshold into the house, thus ushering in fortune.

This is ritual imitative magic; performance to express the desire of the household. The bride is then taken around the house, to each room, she feeds the cow, and stirs the rice and green vegetables being cooked in the kitchen. Rice is a symbol of fortune and green vegetables a symbol of autonomy. Relatives and guests offer gifts when they see the bride the first time (mukh-darshan, muh-dikhai). The bride is also introduced to the family deity (kula-devi) and in Maharashtra there are special ceremonies (gondhal) to entertain the family deity and guests with song and dance.

The marriage may or may not be consummated immediately. Bollywood has made famous the honeymoon night (suhaag raat) where on a perfumed bed bedecked with flowers, the bride awaits, and the groom is locked in by laughing women of his household. She is expected to offer him almond milk, and he is expected to raise her veil (ghoonghat). The veil is prevalent only in North India not South India. Many assume that Muslims brought the veil to India, however it is in all probability a practice that came with Sakas who came from Central Asia to India over 2000 years ago, and who eventually became Hinduized. Reference to women wearing a garment to cover their head and face has been found in Sanskrit literature (Mricchakatika) of the Gupta period, and in Mahayana Buddhist literature (Lalitavistara sutra) too. The word ghoonghat comes from the Sanskrit avagunthan.

10. Registration

India's diversity is evident when one realizes that marriages can be registered with the Indian state using various marriage acts: for Hindus (polygamy forbidden, performed as per cultural practice), for Muslims (polygamy permitted, contractual), for Christians (conducted by the Church, contractual), for Parsis (conducted by Parsi priest, contractual). Buddhists and Jains and tribal weddings are all subsumed within the Hindu Marriage Act. The Sikhs wanted to distinguish themselves, especially to avoid confusion about their faith in other countries, and so now have Anand Marriage Act (conducted before the Guru Granth Sahib, by an Amritdhari priest). And those who do not want a religious wedding, or who belong to two different religions, there is the option of the Special Marriage Act.

The registration of marriage by the Indian State makes all wedding rituals stage performances to satisfy emotions and beliefs of the people involved, good to have but not essential. Registration transforms a stranger into an official member of the family, with rights in social and economic matters, from taking health decisions, to staking a claim on the property. The Indian State privileges the family over friends, especially in case of disputed wills, which is why registration of marriage becomes significant for same-sex couples, even though many Hindu

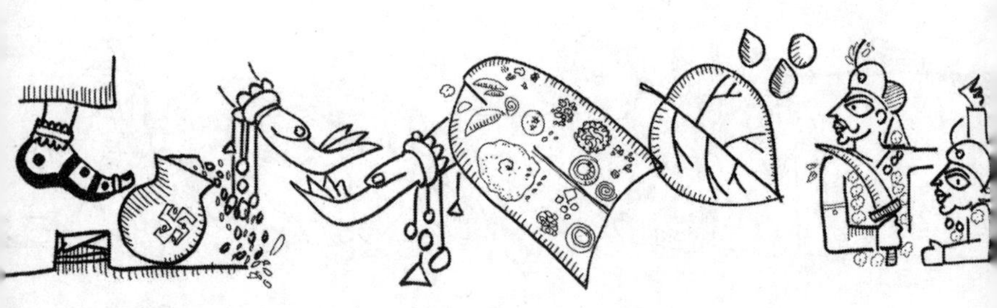

temples and priests are open to the idea of men marrying men and women marrying women.

While Hindu rituals always saw marriage as union of non-gendered souls, wrapped in gendered bodies, the Indian State continues to focus on gendered bodies. Clearly, there is scope for the Indian State to catch up with social realities of the twenty-first century, just as it caught up with ideas such as divorce, and remarriage, in the twentieth century. Courts are still confused between age of (sexual) consent, with age of marriage, as people still assume that boys and girls wait for marriage for their first sexual experience.

Indian state often assumes tradition is fixed and rigid. It is not. It also confuses control with power, rather than insecurity. A grounding in the ancient (shashwat), eternal (sanatan) and infinite (ananta) wisdom of India will enable them to see marriage as the ritual of love, so that they remove all obstacles to the union of any two, mature and willing souls.

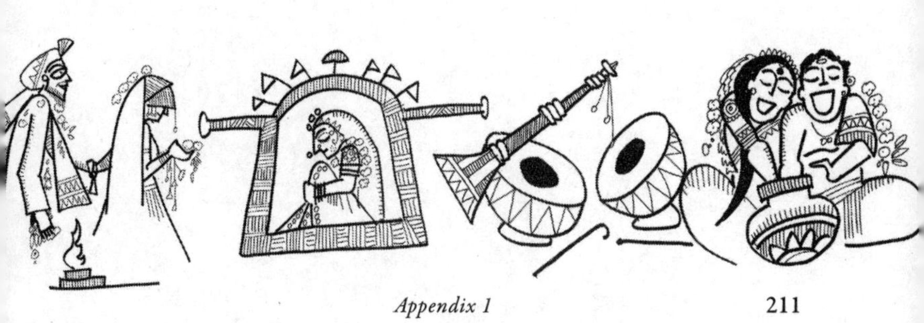

Appendix 2: Oldest Wedding Hymn from the Vedas

'Truth binds the earth (Prithvi) below, and the sun (Aditya) above, and amongst the stars, the moon (Soma), that none can consume, that waxes and wanes with time, guarded by the wind (Vayu). That moon, Soma, was the first husband, guarded by Vayu. For him, the Ashwin twins, wooed Suriya, daughter of the sun (Savitur).

'When Surya agreed, Savitur gave her to Soma. She was led to her husband through fire (Agni). She travelled on a wagon made of her mind. Verse (Rig Veda) and tune (Sama Veda) were the oxen. Earth and Heaven were the wheels of her chariot. Breath served as the axle.'

'Let us salute the gods, Mithra and Varuna, sun and moon, who divide time and seasons, and create order, again and again, bringing things back, as they circulate ceremonially around this altar like playful children.

'Here comes the bride, for her husband. So Vishwavasu, mighty Gandharva, go to those other women, who in father's house still await husbands. Let this woman go to her chosen husband. You are now released from the fetters of your father's house. Now go safely and be mistress of your husband's household, where you will bear good sons and good fortune. With this husband unite your body, and may you always be fair as a couple in distributing household wealth. When he stains your garment red, know that he is now part of your magic, and is ensnared.

'Let the negativity of people that come to the wedding, return with those who brought them. Let no highway robbers attack this wedding party. Let this couple not face hostilities, or obstacles. Much is cut up for the feast of the wedding; let the priest make it all auspicious.

'I, the husband, grasp your hand for good fortune, for the gods including Aryaman and Bhaga have given you to me, and may you grow old with me as your husband, you who roused by Pushan have parted your thighs and let me enter you. You were first acquired by Soma, then by the Gandharva, then Agni, and now you are with me, who by grace will live for a hundred autumns.

'Stay here, you two, ever together, never apart, with children and grandchildren, rejoicing in your own house. Let Prajapati bring progeny into this household. Let Aryaman be with you in old age. Come wife into the world of the husband, bringing joy to his birds and animals, without evil eye or quarrels, of good mind and energy.

'Make this woman, Indra, the bearer of good sons and good fortune. Give her ten sons, let her husband be the eleventh. Be the sovereign queen over your father-in-law and your mother-in-law, your sisters-in-law and your brothers in law. Let the gods and the waters join you together. Let the gods, the director and the disposer, join you together.'

- This is a paraphrased reading of the Rig Veda X.85 wedding hymn.
- Translating any Vedic hymn is difficult as we do not know what to take literally, and what to take metaphorically,

and it is not clear always to whom they are addressed, and who addresses them (this was known to the priests and performers 3000 years ago, of course). Its cryptic nature makes it difficult to understand, though we get a sense of what is happening.

- The hymn begins with the celestial realms and gradually ends with the household. Thus the cosmic is made mundane.

- The wedding was an important ceremony for the Arya (noble men, followers of Vedic rituals). This hymn suggests that women were wooed and brought to the husband's house and became mistress of the household, unlike current weddings where the groom comes and claims the bride and takes her away. It is also different from certain traditional South Indian weddings where men came to the bride's house only when called to give her children.

- The tone suggests that the husband is being 'ensnared' and so is now going to be in bondage. It also suggests that the woman has had many suitors, even lovers before, and there are prayers that she will be satisfied with the husband. The husband is called the eleventh son of the wife; and she is identified as sovereign.

Bibliography

Banerjee, Debjani (translated). Bishnupada Chakravarty. *The Penguin Companion to the Mahabharata*. Penguin India, 2007.

Dange, Sadashiv Ambadas. *Encyclopaedia of Puranic Beliefs and Practices, Vol. 1–5*. New Delhi: Navrang, 1990.

Danielou, Alain. *Gods of Love and Ecstasy: The Traditions of Shiva and Dionysus*. Rochester, Vt.: Inner Traditions International, 1992.

— *Hindu Polytheism*. Rochester, Vt.: Inner Traditions International, 1991.

Gupta, Shakti M. *Plants Myths and Traditions in India*. Delhi: Munishram, New 2013.

Haskar, A. N. D.. *Seduction of Siva: Tales of Life and Love*. Delhi: Penguin, 2014.

Hawley, J. S. and D.M. Wulff, Eds.. *The Divine Consort*. Boston: Beacon Press, 1982.

Hiltebeitel, Alf, ed. *Criminal Gods and Demon Devotees*. New York: State University of New York Press, 1989.

Hiltebeitel, Alf. *Cult of Draupadi, Vol I*. Chicago: University of Chicago Press, 1988.

Hopkins, E. Washburn. *Epic Mythology*. Delhi: Motilal Banarsidass, 1986.

Jakimowicz-Shah, Marta. *Metamorphosis of Indian Gods*. Calcutta: Seagull Books, 1988.

Jamison, Stephanie W., and Joel P. Brereton. *Rigveda: The Earliest Religious Poetry of India. 3 Vols.*, Oxford: Oxford University Press, 2014.

Jayakar, Pupul. *The Earth Mother*. Delhi: Penguin Books, 1989.

Kinsley, David. *Hindu Goddesses*. Delhi: Motilal Banarsidass, 1987.

Knappert, Jan. *An Encyclopedia of Myth and Legend: Indian Mythology*. New Delhi: HarperCollins, 1992.

Mani, Vettam. *Puranic Encyclopaedia*. Delhi: Motilal Banarsidass, 1996.

Mazumdar, Subash. *Who Is Who in the Mahabharata*. Mumbai: Bharatiya Vidya Bhavan, 1988.

Meyer, Johann Jakob. *Sexual Life in Ancient India*. Delhi: Motilal Banarsidass, 1989.

O'Flaherty, Wendy Doniger, trans. *Hindu Myths*. Delhi: Penguin Books, 1975.

— *Origins of Evil in Hindu Mythology*. New Delhi: Motilal Banarsidass, 1988.

— *The Rig Veda: An Anthology*. New Delhi: Penguin Books, 1994.

O'Flaherty, Wendy Doniger. *Sexual Metaphors and Animal Symbols in Indian Mythology*. New Delhi: Motilal Banarsidass, 1981.

— *Śiva: The Erotic Ascetic*. London: Oxford University Press Paperbacks, 1981.

Pandey, Rajbali. *Hindu Samskaras*. Delhi: Motilal Banarsidass, 1969.

Sen, Makhan Lal. *The Ramayana of Valmiki*. Delhi: Munshiram Manoharlal, 1978.

Subramaniam, Kamala. *Srimad Bhagavatam*. Mumbai: Bharatiya Vidya Bhavan, 1987.

— *Mahabharata*. Mumbai: Bharatiya Vidya Bhavan, 1988.

—*Ramayana*. Mumbai: Bharatiya Vidya Bhavan, 1992.

Varadpande, ML. *Mahabharata in Performance*. Clarion Books, 1990

Walker, Benjamin. *Hindu World, Vol 1 and 2*. Delhi: Munshiram Manoharlal, 1983.

Wilkins, W. J. *Hindu Mythology*. Delhi: Rupa Publications, 1997.

Other books by Devdutt Pattanaik

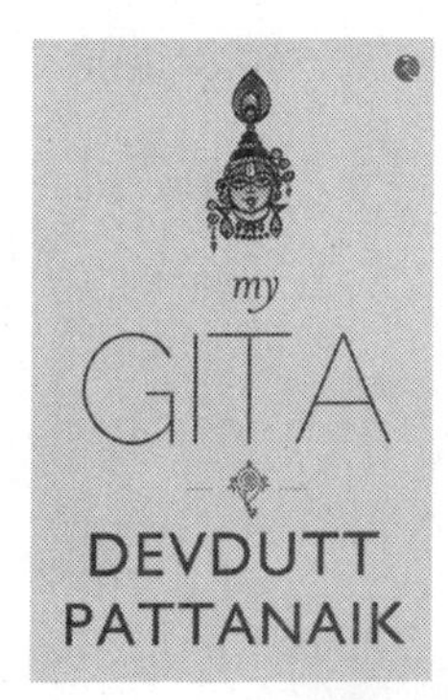

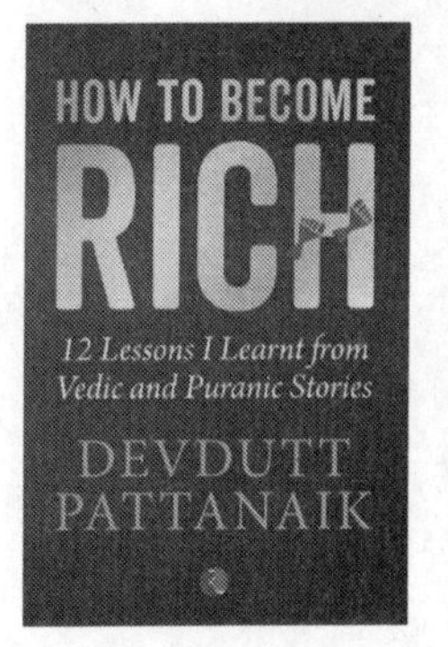